Preface

A library trip to the Duke University in 2014 was unforgettable. CNKI (China National Knowledge Infrastructure hosted by Qinghua University) was then not readily accessible in the United States, and I had to use a specified terminal in the Duke Library to reach for it. When I entered "film, crazy stone" as my key words, the sheer quantity of articles retrieved genuinely amazed me. That was my entry into a rich network of discourses in connection to this film and to a cinematic craziness. This mini book is a result of that entry.

This library trip took place soon after I was appointed to hold Herring Endowed Chair in Asian Studies and Film Studies at Furman University. The endowed fund greatly facilitated my research trips and conference attending in connection with this mini book project. I remain indebted to this source of support.

An earlier, shorter version of current Introduction is published in *Theoretical Studies in Literature and Art,* a Shanghai-based academic journal ("The Neo-noir *Crazy Stone* Phenomenon." *Theoretical Studies in Literature and Art,* 37.2 (2017): 102–117). The current section on film *Happy* in Chap. 3 contains parts of a published article ("Forrest Gump Becomes a Chinese Film Director: Idealism, Formalism and an In-between Audience," *Global Studies Journal,* 8.1 (2015): 1–11). In 2018, I delivered a key-note speech, "*Crazy Stone* Phenomenon in the Perspective of Neo-noir Networking" at the 3rd International Conference on Social Sciences and Humanities in Hangzhou, China.

Appreciation goes to Ann Barrington, who continued to help me edit my language, and to my students of film classes at Furman University, who have sampled Chinese cinematic craziness with warm reception.

Greenville, SC, USA   Harry H. Kuoshu

CONTENTS

About the Author

Harry H. Kuoshu is Herring Professor of Asian Studies and Film Studies at Furman University. He is the author of *Metro Movies: Cinematic Urbanism in Post-Mao China* (2011), *Celluloid China: Cinematic Encounters with Culture and Society* (2002), and *Lightness of Being in China: Adaptation and Discursive Figuration in Cinema and Theater* (1999).

LIST OF FIGURES

CHAPTER 1

Introduction: *Crazy Stone* Phenomenon and Chinese Neo-noir Comedies

Abstract This chapter functions as an introduction to this mini book, which focuses on the postmodern *Crazy Stone* phenomenon emerged in recent Chinese cultural and cinematic scenes. It explores the implications of a black carnival to the contemporary Chinese; the resources of being crazy in Chinese culture; the meanings of modernism and postmodernism to the Chinese; the making of darkness in relation to black humor and film noir; the role of laughter, nihilism, and cynicism in producing the sense of darkness; and how a carnival kind of craziness characterizes contemporary Chinese culture and becomes the context of today's film production, criticism, and reception. The study argues that the *Crazy Stone* phenomenon is part of the global neo-noir, which is an important topic in film and cultural studies scholarship that has for long missed the China component.

Keywords Craziness • Carnival • Postmodernism • Modernism • Film noir • Neo-noir • Black humor • Laughter • Nihilism • Cynicism

© The Author(s), under exclusive license to Springer Nature Switzerland AG 2021
H. H. Kuoshu, *Craziness and Carnival in Neo-Noir Chinese Cinema*, Chinese Literature and Culture in the World, https://doi.org/10.1007/978-3-030-73081-9_1

1

1   BLACK CARNIVAL: THE STONE PHENOMENON

In 2006, the Chinese film market was promoting Zhang Yimou's *Curse of the Golden Flower* and Feng Xiaogang's *The Banquet*. Zhang and Feng were both big names in China but their high-budget, glossy, stardom-supported adaptation of well-known classics, as if echoing Chen Kaige's popularly jeered film *The Promise* of the previous year, met with an unsympathetic audience.[1] The reigning Hollywood blockbuster films of the year were *Poseidon* and *Ice Age 2*; they also generated weak box office income. Into this lukewarm market, galloped a black horse. It was *Crazy Stone* (Fengkuang de shitou) by a twenty-nine-year-old director Ning Hao, who graduated from Beijing Film Academy in 2003 and his earlier films, such as *Incents* and *Mongolian Ping Pong*, were all low-budget but artistically successful and popular films. Andy Lau, a Hong Kong actor/singer/producer, invested in this talented Shanxi native of Ning Hao with his "New Star Directors of Asia" program. The release of *Crazy Stone* caused quite a stir in the market. The film, with an investment of three million RMB, should still be considered a low-budget one. It, nonetheless, drew the audience away from the blockbusters and in a month's time generated a box office income of fifteen million. The audience so liked the film that comments on the film online were often tagged by hundreds of responding comments. Scholars also cheered the popularity of the film. Culturally, a "stone phenomenon" was produced, which was remembered as the popular indulgence in craziness in 2006. That July, film producers and scholars gathered at the Chinese Filmmakers' Association to discuss this film at a session entitled "*Crazy Stone*: A Black Carnival" (Fig. 1.1). They believed that the film would serve as an index to "film production trends of the era that people had already had some vague sense of but had not had the chance to categorize" (Wu Guanping et al. 2006, 73). Indeed, in the following years, discourse about this film did exactly that, categorizing the cultural implications of the *Crazy Stone* phenomenon.

Crazy Stone tells an absurd story of a most precious piece of jade being rediscovered at an unlikely place: a broken toilet in a struggling factory that is slated for demolition. The value of the stone may save the factory and the livelihood of its employees. Yet it also lures thieves, including one sent by an unethical real estate developer who wants the land the factory occupies and a group of con men dreaming of the big time. The film is prompted by the pressing social issues of the real estate-fueled economic growth versus the anxiety experienced by laid-off workers. The film's

Fig. 1.1 *Crazy Stone*. A black carnival

biting satire, nonetheless, is a comic tug-of-war between the amateur, factory-appointed jade protection crew (headed by security chief Bao), and a mixture of all sorts of would-be jade thieves.

Although the film's producers and fans of the film avoided discussing the allegory of the film, critics cannot help but compare *Crazy Stone* to an eighteenth-century literary masterpiece, *The Story of the Stone* (Honglou meng), in which a piece of jade becomes the core of an allegory. Here, the allegory is that of desire and human responses to it—scholar Wang Guowei has pointed out that jade and desire are both pronounced as *yu* in Chinese. Like the novel, *Crazy Stone* features a similar quest for truth hidden in absurdity. While *The Story of the Stone* has long attracted critical and scholarly attention, *Crazy Stone* is becoming a similarly compelling work. Cross-culturally, *Crazy Stone* is also seen as a Sinicized parody of the myth of Sisyphus, especially as the absurdist philosopher Albert Camus describes the tale in his 1942 essay, and in the way Sisyphus is remembered locked into an eternal, futile struggle of rolling an immense boulder up a hill, only to watch it roll back down. In this comparison, *Crazy Stone* has become a vivid indicator of the vague, widespread sense of absurdity shared by contemporary Chinese.

To be crazy is to join this cultural carnival of 2006. *Crazy Stone* was figuratively thrown into a societal and cultural pond and became the center of impacting ripples. The number of similarly titled films is impressive enough to show its impact. In 2009, Nin Hao directed *Crazy Racer* (Fengkuang de saiche), another popular film that also broke the box-office record. In 2010, the Fourth Generation director Huang Jianzhong was inspired by the ripples of the craziness and aided a younger director, Lang Chen, in producing *Crazy Necklace* (Fengkuang de xianglian), a detective story about the theft of an expensive necklace that eventually leads to the exposure of commercial bribery and government corruption. The producers of this film well realized that craziness had become a catchy word in marketing—they invited potential investors to "have a journey accompanied by craziness."[2] In 2012, Shang Jing directed *Crazy Dinner Party* (Fanju ye fengkuang) for the Chinese New Year season. With multiple story lines and a comic style, this suspenseful film revealed diversified motives of all those involved in a dinner party which also becomes the scene of a murder. In the same year, Li Kai combined actors from *Crazy Stone* and actors known for Hong Kong gangster films to make *Crazy, Stupid Thieves* (Fengkuang de chunzei). In 2013, Song Yang directed *Crazy Director* (Fengkuang de daoyan), exposing the cruel reality of the filmmaking world in a style of absurdity and self-mockery. By 2014, just as the attraction of crazy-titled comedies had begun to wane, an award-winning art director with limited popular appeal joined the trend with commercial success. Li Jixian showcased *Nights of Adventure*, literally "Crazy 72 Hours" (Fengkuang qishier xiaoshi), which refers to Ning Hao's *Crazy Stone* in story, sources of inspiration, and style.

In producing the cultural ripples of craziness, Ning Hao's pioneering role was not accidental; he actually helped engineering it. In 2010, Ning Hao was joined by scriptwriter Ning Caishen (literally "Monetary God Ning") and Shanghai based play director He Nian. The three of them adapted Ning Hao's film *Crazy Racer* into a play and staged it at Beijing's prestigious Capital Theater. The title of the play remained focused on the message they intended to send out: *Crazy Show* (Fengkuang de fengkuang). The poster for the show described their message in a threefold way: (1) to let *avant-garde* artists cross disciplines to experiment the newest edition of crazy editing, (2) to quickly delete the audience's old memories of watching a play, and (3) to let audience go crazy in a vigorous game and indulgent fun. The event, in the name of *avant-garde*, would be most appropriate to occur in the Capital Theater, which has been serving as the cradle for Chinese experimentalism in theater. In a different perspective, however, the event could also be seen as a challenge; whereas the earlier experimentalism staged here are primarily events of high culture, *Crazy Show* is popular culture's invasion to this sacred place with an earnest request to reconsider the boundary between high culture and popular culture, serious art, and entertainment. *Crazy Show,* one needs to know, was produced by three box office champions of the time. Ning Caishen's fame is built on the script he wrote for Shang Jing's 2011 film *My Own Swordsman* (Wulin waizhuan), which has a box office income of 200 million *yuan.* He Nian is known in the theater world as a "box office honey." In 2010, his play *The Capital* (Ziben lun), named after Karl Marx's book and dramatizing the impact of contemporary financial crisis, won him not only a theater prize but also the box office income as high as 165 million *yuan.* In comparison, the film that brought these people together, *Crazy Racer,* had only 100 million box office income.

The impact of 2006 carnival can also be detected in popular culture. Again, one can use the phrase *fengkuang* (craziness) as a clue. Since 2006, over twenty episodes of a comic video series *Migrant Workers Are Also Crazy* (Mingong ye fengkuang) have been uploaded online and have a hitting rate of over a billion times. In 2006, a twenty-one-episode TV series was titled *Ugly Girls Are Also Crazy* (Chounü ye fengkuang). In 2011, Souhu Media Inc. issued a ten-episode TV series *Crazy Office* (Fengkuang de bangongshi), featuring a small-time CEO Opama's struggle in keeping his Crazy Dream Company from sinking. In 2012 Xi'an Shulin Media Company issued a TV series *Woman Chef is Also Crazy* (Zhufu ye fengkuang). *Fengkuang* even shows up in restaurant names. In 2007, a chain restaurant known as "Crazy Roasted Wings" (fengkuang kaochi) was established in Beijing and claimed online that its popularity could compete with either the cyber star Sister Hibiscus (furong jiejie) or the comic show star Guo Degang. The phrase *fengkuang* is also frequently adopted in translation. The 2010 American film *The Back-up Plan* is translated as *The Left-over Girls are also Crazy* (Shengnü ye fengkuang). The 2013 American 3D film *The Croods* was translated as *Crazy Primitives* (Fengkuang yuanshiren). In 2014, a Japanese gaming TV program was dubbed first as *Crazy Stone* and then *Crazy Maigi.* A popular electronic game "Angry Birds" is known as "Crazy Birds" (Fengkuang de xiaoniao) in Chinese. "Crazy Fishing" (Fengkuang puyu) and "Crazy Bull Fighting" (Fengkuang douniu) are other popular electronic games. *Crazy Darlings* (Fengkuang baobei) constitute a type of characters in Chinese virtual games. China's pop singer Chris Lee (Li Yuchun), who was featured on the cover of the *Time* magazine in America in 2005, has an extremely popular album titled *Be Crazy before We're Too Old* (Zai bu fengkuang women jiu lao le).

Identifying the 2006 field of ripples, one is reminded of another center of ripples also featuring craziness well over a decade ago, when film director Zhou Xiaowen produced his films *Desperation* (literally, Last Craziness, 1987) and *Obsession* (literally, The Price for Craziness, 1988). Other contemporary films, such as Liu Guoquan's *Desperate Songstress* (literally, Crazy Songstress / Fengkuang genü, 1990), also bore testimony to the influence of the craziness then. Although the word craziness did not prop up in that many film titles then, it was still an eye-catching word frequently picked up by film critics. A 1996 book on director Zhou Xiaowen reflected this discursive focus with the title *"Xiaowen ye fengkuang"* (Xiaowen Is Equally Crazy). Comparing with the critical reception of *Crazy Stone*, Zhou's crazy-titled films were also hailed as a breakthrough, initially that of the rigid distinction between commercial films (shangye pian) and art films (yishu pian), but soon with more underpinnings discovered by critics and scholars. What of interest is that we encounter two ripple centers both featuring craziness and both denoting deviation, breakthrough, or rebellion. Their comparison may spell out layers of changes in Chinese cultural and cinematic discourses. At start, however, one needs to look into cultural implications of the concept of craziness to see if its layers of historical configuration and performances in cultural scenes may help understand its current usage.

2   DOG AND KING: TO CONFIGURE CRAZINESS

The etymology of *feng* and *kuang*, the two Chinese characters that form the modern Chinese phrase of crazy/craziness/craze/mad/madness but were in ancient times also used separately, opens up various channels for understanding their usage. Character *feng* appears rather late in history, roughly since the Sung dynasty (Ye Shuxian 1999, 42). It contains the disease radical in its formation. It is thus about illness and indicates the mind's invasion by an unpleasant natural element in air known as "wind" (feng). A mad person is one who has lost his mind's balancing capacity to remain normal.

Whereas *feng* has more a pathological implication, the other ancient character of *kuang* brings in the social and cultural elements in etymology. The original meaning of *kuang*, according to Han dynasty etymologist Xu Shen, refers to "the crazy dog." The formation of the character has a meaning indicator of "dog" and a sound indicator of "king." Considering the historical usages of *kuang*, however, I would rather take the character as a hybrid one: it combines two independent characters of "dog" and "king." The "dog" part of the character indicates a member of certain groups of social animals who is tempted to challenge the other part of the character, "the king," or the head of the group. *Kuang* thus indicates anti-social behaviors. A close relative to *kuang* in anti-social implication is the character *guang* (wandering, exile), which combines the movement radical and the character of king. *Guang* is an exile from the king or social norms. Etymologically, the modern phrase *fengkuang* denotes such concepts of psychology (normal/abnormal), social order (acceptance/rebellion), and cultural formation (center/margin)—the implications of all of which may change with time. In this article, I choose to use the English word crazy/craziness to refer to *fengkuang* but occasionally switch to mad/madness when the context calls for them.

Ancient Chinese depiction of craziness shows a binary conception: *kuang* for action and *juan*, an ancient character that did not find new life in any modern phrases, for contemplation, as shown in Confucius saying that "*Kuang* is for achievement and *juan* aims at non-action."[3] Since Confucian ideal is the rational, social action guided by the principle of decorum, craziness (kuang juan) is considered a complementary or secondary option to rational thoughts and actions. In contrast, the founders of Taoism, who are anti-government and are thus less concerned with social discipline, would be less reserved about craziness, believing it to be almost the natural status of human life not yoked by artificiality. This concept is shown in Zhuangzi's praise of the innocent citizens of a Taoist society that their "free action of craziness is actually the endowment of grand nature," that "such kind of life is happy," and that "death in such life causes no regret."[4]

Du Fu, the Tang dynasty social critic and poet, helps illustrate an ancient artistic use of craziness. Known for his uncompromising sternness in exposé and cultural criticism in his poetry, Du Fu uses the phrase of "three craziness" (san kuang) to characterize his own poetry writing career: crazy wandering (kuang zou), crazy perception (kuang gu), and crazy songs (kuang ge). Here, the Chinese word *kuang* indicates the poet's self-consciousness that he is a rebel to the conventional political views, and that he is culturally and politically an exile. Du Fu's self-portrayal leads us to see a category of ancient Chinese intelligentsia who dared to be critics. It is just as what Yu Yingshi observes in his book *Shi Scholars and Chinese Culture*,

> There is a category of *kuang shi* (crazy scholar) in Chinese history; *kuang* has to do with telling truth. Lord Guangwu is recorded [in *Chronicle of History*] quoting a set phrase circulated between Qin and Han dynasties, "a sage king knows to listen to crazy persons." This saying indicates that *kuang* and candid opinions are synonyms then. (Yu Yingshi 1987, 116)

Du Fu's phrase of crazy wandering is especially interesting since it vindicates the etymological relatedness of *kuang* and *guang* (wandering, exile) as mentioned before. It also reminds one of contemporary critical concept of *flânerie* as used, for example, by Anke Gleber in *The Art of Taking a Walk: Flânerie, Literature, and Film in Weimar Culture*. The concept denotes forms of spatial practice adopted by European intelligentsia as subversive tactics to combat alienation in urban life in the West. Ancient Tang and modern Europe showcased similar spatial practice shown in the identical forms of walking or self-imposed exile, understanding through observing and expressing criticism.

Du Fu's contemporary poet Li Bai also depicted himself as a "crazy man" (kuang ren) in his well-known line "I am by nature a Chu crazy man, / In phoenix songs jeer at Confucius." In his case, *kuang* also had anti-social implications. Li Bai's glorious time in court was achieved not by going through national civil service examinations but by his reputation for poetry and by producing such legends while "crazy" from inebriation. He demands that the emperor stir his soup, the consort hold the ink-stone for him, and the chief eunuch remove his boots: "he wouldn't respond to the Emperor's summon, claiming that he is the wine god" (according to Du Fu's poetic depiction). His whole crazy-man poem is a eulogy of nature (phoenix songs) against the court (Confucius). *Kuang* in Li Bai's case, nonetheless, leads people to think more of his unique poetic talent. *Kuang*, in this sense, can very well be Li Bai's "muse," what the ancient Greek philosopher Socrates describes as "a divinely inspired release from normally accepted behavior" (Bussanich and Smith 2013, 277).

In *Phaedrus*, Plato recorded Socrates' taxonomy of four types of madness: (1) prophetic madness inspired by Apollo, (2) telesic or ritual madness induced by Dionysus, (3) poetic madness inspired by the Muses, and (4) erotic madness aroused by Eros and Aphrodite (Bussanich and Smith 277). Socrates believes that "madness from a god is finer than self-control of human origin" and produces "fine achievements" and "good fortune" (Bussanich and Smith 2013, 277). In Chinese ancient shamanistic tradition, as Qu Yuan's anthology *Songs of Chu* revealed, madness (achieved in a state of trance) was a vehicle of communicating with gods. However, the generally non-religious nature of the Chinese culture has kept it from producing any discussion of madness as religious experience as Socrates does. Chinese culture, nonetheless, leaves room for creative craziness intuitively, believing that craziness is an indication of supreme wisdom. This intuition is best shown in the ancient Chinese saying "*dazhi si kuang*" (supreme wisdom appears crazy).

While Li Bai fashioned himself as a crazy man in a previous era, Lu Xun's fictional characterization of craziness, especially that in his story "Diary of a Madman," offers us a modern example of craziness for cultural critique. Lu Xun's literary use of craziness may be traced to the Taoist tradition of "*you fang zhi wai*" (traveling beyond the mundane) and "*duyu tiandi jinshen wanglai*" (establishing a unique connection with the wisdom endowed in nature). Yet, more important for a modern writer, Lu Xun's madman demonstrates cross-cultural influences. His "Diary of a Madman" was obviously inspired by Russian writer Nikolai Gogol's story of the same title, and it shares the critical edge shown in Gogol's grotesque writing, which for both Gogol and Lu Xun functions as the "means of estranging" and "a comic hyperbole that unmasks the banality and inhumanity of ambient reality" (Fusso 1994, 55). The meaning of madness in Lu Xun's madman was also derived from German philosopher Friedrich Nietzsche, a major source of Lu Xun's intellectual inspiration. Here the madness has to do with Dionysian intoxication and ecstasy, which are capable of the liberation of instinct and dissolution of boundaries. Madness of this kind may generate wisdom that those imprisoned by the reigning cultural values are not capable of understanding right away— it is just like Nietzsche's madman who claims to have arrived too early for others to understand him. In his writing, Lu Xun constructed a similar confrontation as his madman faces a pathetic Chinese cultural status quo, "an iron house without windows, absolutely indestructible, with many people fast asleep inside who will soon die of suffocation" (1977, 5).

In addition to being a unique perspective in contemplation, craziness also involves a sense of theater. Just like Nietzsche's madman needs to draw a crowd in the marketplace to shock, the action of craziness always achieves its social effect by drawing and maintaining an audience. If culture is performative, as maintained by many theorists, craziness disrupts the accepted codes of performance and relies on this disruption for its own visibility. In our survey of the historical conception of craziness, it is important to note, we can see that the actors are primarily individuals and their "theaters" small. In contrast, the *Crazy Stone* phenomenon of 2006 captivated a vast number of moviegoers. As many Chinese critics quickly realized, it is a carnival, or rather the carnival as Mikhail Bakhtin defines one in his *Rabelais and His World*. The way American-based scholar Zuyan Zhou uses Bakhtin's conception of carnival to analyze the classical Chinese novel, *Journey to the West*, is relevant to our study of the *Crazy Stone* phenomenon. As Zhou shows us, Bakhtin takes carnival as a "communal patterning of imagination," a "gay relativity," a freedom in "visualizing the world and men," and a way of employing laughter as "a powerful support for storming the stronghold of the Gothic Age" (1994, 69–70). In his conception, Bakhtin forcefully illustrates carnival as a "critical metaphor" and a literary apparatus with specific formal features. Zhou successfully applies these conceptions to an insightful discussion of *Journey to the West*, using many formalistic details of the novel to prove that "the late Ming novelists' 'obsession' with carnival in Chinese literati novels is, to a certain degree, generated by—as well as mirrors—the ideological ferment of this period" (1994, 70). The "obsession with carnival" is how this example of ancient literary work connects with our topic here. Carnival involves elements of craziness. Compared with our survey, however, carnival also suggests a transit in the locations of culture: from individual perception to communal imagination, from private "theater" to mass revelry, from court (where individual critics draw limited attention) to the marketplace (where mass indulgence may function as protest), and from high culture to popular culture. What is more interesting is that these transits, often the case, indicate the related cultural traffic that connects the high and popular cultures, rather than an indication of their separation. In *Journey to the West*, Chan Buddhism relied on many popular cultural elements to assert its proper position not only in Chinese religious philosophy but also in popular culture. In the *Crazy Stone* phenomenon, we see an interesting alliance of contrasting cultural elements, particularly shown in the élite intellectuals emphasizing the grassroots in scholarly terms.

Craziness is also an aspect of contemporary film culture, as Stephen Farber (1974, 252) observes in his article "Movie Crazy" that "more and more films seem to be drawn from other films rather than from life." In "pastiches of bits and pieces drawn from earlier comedies and melodramas" (Farber 1974, 252), this craziness indicates the importance of movie elements, as constituents of popular culture, to generations of folks who grow up with movie-going. In understanding this sort of craziness, a particular Chinese cinematic pastiche known as *egao* (mischievous parody of other films or art works) in 2006 carnival becomes important. *Egao*, around that time, became a popular trend in Chinese mass culture and mass media, characterizing a generally shared rebel gesture of jeering at the sublime. Known as a mass indulgence and pastime, *egao* weaved a network of films mischievously referring to other films in addition to it being a social lubricant in mass communication. As we are going to see in our later discussion, *egao* connects the Chinese carnival with the global neo-noir and it allows Chinese scholars to use the concept of postmodernism to describe the characteristics of this mass participation of a cultural carnival.

3   DARKNESS: BLACK HUMOR, FILM NOIR, AND NEO-NOIR

The *Crazy Stone* phenomenon is known as a black carnival primarily because of the film's infectious black humor, beloved by Chinese audiences and critics alike. The concept of black humor has long been applied to the interpretation of post-Mao Chinese films. Chinese scholars acknowledge that the term was coined by the French surrealist theoretician Andre Breton when he published his *Anthologie de l'humour noir* (anthology of black humor), and the term was used to designate a particular kind of satirical comedy in which laughter was induced by cynicism and skepticism (Xiu Ti 2005). They also acknowledge that American writer Bruce Jay Friedman's volume of the same title rejuvenated the term and promoted its Western use in the 1960s and the 1970s. The implication of the term here, according to a Chinese scholar, is "buffoonery plus horror":

> The author can see funniness in horror, produce crazy, chilling laughter at the absurdity of the world, so as to reduce the nameless, existential anxiety and its suffocating sense of oppression. (Xiu Ti 2005, 118)

Another Chinese scholar emphasizes the "existential absurdity and chill" of the term, detailing it as "helpless jeering at traditional values and aesthetics, showcasing of alienation, loss of humanities, and the shattering of feelings" (Xi Yongfeng 2006, 4). *Catch-22*, the satirical novel by the American author Joseph Heller, laid the foundation of the popular appeal of this term in China since the absurdity referred to in this story is well known through translation: You can be discharged from the army if you are crazy. However, you have to apply for discharge, and applying demonstrates that you are not crazy. As a result, you will never be discharged.

The Chinese, having experienced social unrest and cultural dislocation since the chaotic decade of the Cultural Revolution (1966–1976), are drawn by the zeitgeist connoted in the American genre of black humor: McCarthyism, civil rights movements, anti-Vietnam war campaigns, college campus unrest, drug use, and anti-cultural trends. In China, a reviewer may use the black humor label when a film uses humor that induces both laughter and tears, and the humor reflects post-Mao political and cultural frustration. Huang Jianxin's 1985 film *Black Cannon Incident* has commonly been considered a classical example of the genre. The absurdity of the film derives from how a trivial thing in life, an engineer sending a telegram to retrieve his lost chess piece, induces a chain of political responses: he is suspected of espionage, removed from his job, and secretly investigated. The events unfold like the workings of an obsolete machine— it is out of date, alienated, runs by habit, and ultimately destructive. The behavior of the characters in the film is both absurd and sincere, indicating a deep-rooted ideological condition that renders people helpless. The film's "modernist" techniques, such as striking color symbolism and allegorical *mise en scène*, help polarize the dark vision of the film and the absurdity of its expression. Joining *Black Cannon Incident*, other black humor films include several of Huang's later films such as *Dislocation* (Cuowei, 1986) and *Surveillance* (Maifu, 1997), Xie Jin's *Hibiscus Town* (Furong zhen, 1986), Mi Jiashan's *The Troubleshooters* (Wanzhu, 1988), Zhang Yimou's *To Live* (Huo zhe, 1994), Jiang Wen's *Devils on the Doorstep* (Guizi laile, 2000), Lu Chuan's *The Missing Gun* (Xun qiang, 2002), Cao Baoping's *Troublemakers* (Guang rong de fennu, 2006), and Guan Hu's *Cow* (Dou niu, 2009). These films showcase identity crises and problems with political culture and feature the nationalist characters in extreme, absurd situations.

While becoming widely used in Chinese film criticism and scholarship, the concept of black humor actually suppresses discussion of film noir, which is written about but rarely applied to an actual analysis of Chinese films, as if black humor can fully explain issues related to darkness. In the "black carnival" of the *Crazy Stone*, the concept of black humor is frequently activated from the start in accessing this and the related films. Concerning the frequent use of black humor in this discourse, one Chinese scholar (Chen Hongxiu 2012) raises concerns about the concept's over-usage and proposes the need to distinguish black humor from black comedy. According to Chen, black humor and black comedy are two Sinicized genres claiming different sources: the former, as indicated earlier, derives from American black humor literature, and the latter derives, more to the point of our discussion here, from the genre of American film noir since the 1940s. Other differences follow in her discussion: (1) in subject, black humor favors war and politics and black comedy is interested in gangsters and underground societies; (2) in their connection to the humanity traditions, whereas black humor is influenced by existentialist philosophies and its protests concern uncertainty about established beliefs in human nature and social order, black comedy has less metaphysical underpinnings and aims more at the pleasure of rebellion; (3) black humor delves more into the consciousness of the main characters whereas black comedy offers fewer glimpses into the minds of the characters; and (4) black humor uses the rather traditional pattern of narrative with often just one story line whereas black comedy uses unconventional narrative, often with multiple story lines and diversified narrative perspectives (Chen Hongxiu 2012, 180). To this scholar, films inspired by *Crazy Stone* should all be categorized as black comedy (i.e., the Chinese offspring of Western film noir) instead of black humor.

From Chen's argument, we may come up with two initial assumptions: first, what keeps the concept of film noir from surfacing in criticism and scholarship may well be due to a Chinese perception that the concept is not philosophically as profound as black humor, and second, this absence may also be due to the related perception that characters portrayed in the films of this genre are often too shallow to be interesting.

The first assumption clearly indicates the lack of an informed and comprehensive enough understanding of film noir. Film noir, as James Naremore states, "belongs to the history of ideas as much as to the history of cinema" (1995–96, 14). It refers both to a group of films and the discourse about these films, and it may refer to a period, a Zeitgeist, a style, a genre, a mood, a movement, or a phenomenon pending on one's emphasis. Here, it is particularly interesting to look at film noir as a phenomenon since our "*Crazy Stone* phenomenon" involves a similar interaction between films and ideas about films. From this perspective, one must emphasize that "the French invented film noir" (1995–96, 15). According to Naremore's study, the French read their wartime experience (often described as *les années noires*) of torture, compromise, and collaboration into the personal style of resistance featured in noir films. The discourse was set in the context of high modernism, which values personal instinct shown in "accents of rebellion" against the "fatality of evil" (1995–96, 17). The importance of existentialism in French intellectual culture is another noticeable influence, intertwined with residual surrealism—"from their beginnings in the years after World War I, the surrealists had used cinema as an apparatus for the destruction of bourgeois art and the desublimation of everyday life" (1995–96, 18). With all these elements involved, it is hard to accept the validity of the claim that film noir is intellectually pale. In addition, film noir should be able to shoulder social and cultural critique as competently as black humor has done in Chinese discourse. Film noir, as Winfried Fluck observes, can be considered an especially attractive form of social and cultural criticism since it is easy "to trace the fate of the main character(s) to the point of entrapment or self-destruction in order to arrive at an easy confirmation of the cruelty of the system" (2001, 382).

The second assumption is also misleading since it has missed a major concern of film noir, that is, the enigmatic psychology of its main characters, into which cultural and psychoanalytic analysis may easily cut. Distinguishing film noir from a gangster film, Fluck points out a major difference between the two: "the crime is no longer committed by a 'professional' criminal but by an 'ordinary' citizen who is drawn—or appears to have been drawn—into crime by accident or some strange, unforeseen combination of factors" (2001, 383). Given this distinction, the narrative focus of film noir often lies on the circumstances that drive the main character into crime, the line between being guilty and not guilty becomes blurred, the moral oppositions get conflated, and the night metaphor, as well as the rhetoric of disillusion and distrust, tends to lead the audience into the dark dimensions of the often-incomprehensible self.

The darkness of this sort, concerning incomprehensible self, is arguably at the core of our three major films I selected for Chap. 2 to showcase the first round of crazy ripples, when Chinese culture was producing its own version of post-Mao modernism. All these films also happen to tell crime stories. If we check them against other characteristics of film noir—involving romanticism or femme fatale, urban setting, unorthodox narration, ambiguity of human motives, and critique of commodity culture—they also fit fairly well. It is not too hard to refer to these films as noir-ish and thus darkness, which has not been emphasized in the reviews of these films, may become a prominent topic for their interpretation. As I am to discuss in that chapter, in these films' accidental resemblance to film noir, one witnesses similar artistic expressions owing to similar cultural needs, a parallelism that is meaningful enough to enhance each other's interpretation but shows no significant communication of influences between related films and the genre. For the films produced in the second round of crazy ripples, as they have already been identified by a Chinese scholar as black comedies, their kinship with film noir is indirectly confirmed.

Nonetheless, the term used in reviews of Chinese films remains to be "black comedy" and not "*heise dianying*" (black film), the literal translation of the ignored film noir. In 2000 and 2001, the indebtedness of Luo Ye's influential film *Suzhou River* (Suzhou he) to Hitchcock's noir film *Vertigo* was highlighted in the programs of several international film festivals (Hong Kong, Rotterdam, and Toronto). Ever since, this topic of interpreting *Suzhou River* in light of film noir was fully established, even in book-length studies, in English language scholarship overseas. The concept of film noir, nonetheless, never surfaced in published scholarship concerning this film in China.[5]

In 2014, when a Chinese thriller *Black Coal, Thin Ice* (Bairi yanhuo) won the Golden Bear award at the 64th Berlin International Film Festival, along with the Western praise of it being "a most curious hybrid of genre movie [film noir] and art film" (Foundas 2014),[6] the concept of film noir started to show up in its reviews in China. One Chinese reviewer's fascination with the concept showed another common misconception,

> Director Diao Yinan produced a *heise dianying* (film noir) with common urban residents in Chinese provincial cities. It is enigmatic to discover that a film genre, which was popular in the west in the past but now almost extinct, would "ferry across oceans" and to "reincarnate" itself in a Chinese film. (Meng Fanxuan 2014, 123)

To many in China, film noir is mistaken as a genre that is long dead. The film noir they refer to here is what I refer to as traditional noir.

Western scholars identify two rounds of film noir discourse, influenced by modernism and postmodernism respectively. Concerning the renewed interest in film noir since the 1970s, Naremore writes,

> A plausible case could indeed be made that, far from dying out with the old studio system, noir is most entirely a creation of postmodern culture—a belated reading of classic Hollywood that was polarized by cinéastes of the French New Wave, appropriated by reviewers, academics, and film-makers, and then recycled on TV. (1995–96, 14)

Fluck also talks about film noir remaining relevant since the discourse features film noir 1 and film noir 2: "Roughly equivalent with the arrival of postmodern culture in the 1960s, that this playful film noir 2 replaced the earlier existentialist form of reception" (2001, 405). For film noir 1, there is the problem of "split subject," which prompts the spectator to wonder how he "can be released from the same fate, that is, from his own repression" (2001, 405). Film noir 2 offers the possibility "to cite this option without having to enter it" since it has become "a cinema without depth" (2001, 405).

David Desser defined this second round of film noir, or neo-noir, as a "global noir," since "what works in New York also works in Brussels, Hong Kong and Tokyo, not to mention London, Paris and Seoul" (2003, 516). Exploring transnational filmmaking and film distribution, global flow of capital, cultural and human resources, as well as the "mediascape"-sustained repertoires of communications about films, Desser has made the case forcefully that this second round of film noir is a global phenomenon. Mediascape, as conceptualized by anthropologist Arjun Appadurai in his *Modernity at Large: Cultural Dimensions of Globalization*, is the globalized spectacle of the expanding cyber/media/lingual world,

> Mediascapes refers both to the distribution of the electronic capabilities to produce and disseminate information (newspapers, magazines, television stations, and film-production studios) ... and to the images of the world created by these media ... What is most important about these mediascapes is that they provide (especially in their television, film, and cassette forms) large and complex repertoires of images, narratives and ethnoscapes [landscapes of people] to viewers throughout the world. (Appadurai 1996, 35)

Defining the global noir with the "impulse toward cinephilia" at its heart, that is, "the ability and necessity of acknowledging the intertextual chain of references, borrowings, and re-workings" (Desser 2003, 528), Desser has positioned a global noir circulating the mediascapes. One wonders, however, if ideological boundaries (embodied historically in the iron curtain, the Berlin wall, the 38th parallel, and "the great firewall of China") may exclude parts of the world from this global phenomenon. After all, Desser has not had the chance to show that what works in New York may also work in Beijing or Moscow or Havana.

As a partial answer to this question, I argue that the *Crazy Stone* phenomenon in China can indeed be considered an episode of the global neo-noir. This phenomenon is created in China, but it is also connected with the global culture that sustains what is known as the neo-noir. Whereas other Asian countries joined the neo-noir as it bloomed in the 1990s, Chinese response was a little delayed. Concerning any local participation of a global phenomenon, its context is at least twofold: that of local culture and society and that of a media-sustained celluloid culture and society; the former may alter or delay the impact of the latter. The reason for the delay in the appearance of Chinese neo-noir has to do with the role played by internet-sustained mediascape. In his *More than Night*, Naremore (2008, 255) suggests that "noir itself is a kind of mediascape—a loosely related collection of perversely mysterious motifs or scenarios that circulate through all the information technologies." When Arjun Appadurai coined the term mediascape in the early 1990s, the internet's role in circulating these materials was only just budding. Without a truly global internet, noir may have been a mediascape in the West prior to the 1990s, but it was definitely not yet in China.

The impact of *Crazy Stone* on other similar films produced in China is very much like that of *Pulp Fiction* on its imitators in the West in the 1990s, even though the immediate Western influence on *Crazy Stone* is that of Guy Ritchie's *Lock, Stock and Two Smoking Barrels* (1998). If *Pulp Fiction* has, as Desser maintains, created a "cycle" of commercially successful films of similar noir styles in the West, *Crazy Stone*, relaying this influence, has produced an alternative cycle in China.

Pulp Fiction has been immensely influential in China. In 1995, Quentin Tarantino visited China, screened this film at a hotel auditorium, and had a panel discussion with students of Beijing Film Academy. One professor noted that Tarantino's visit caused quite a stir among the young Chinese film artists (Hao Jian 2002, 59). Scholarly discussion of *Pulp Fiction* started in the same year, with Sima Xiaolan's introduction of it appearing in *World Cinema* and Hao Jian's translation of its script being published in *Contemporary Film*. In the following years, many scholarly articles on *Pulp Fiction* and its director appeared. He Jianjun's film *Pirated Copy* (Manyan, 2004) testifies to *Pulp Fiction*'s popular reception in China; a character in this Chinese film appears to be possessed by a character from *Pulp Fiction* and acts just like him and utters his exact signature phrases in a crisis situation. Jia Zhangke is also a big fan of *Pulp Fiction,* and several of his films reflect the popularity of *Pulp Fiction* with Chinese youth. If Jia Zhangke's pastiche of *Pulp Fiction* in his *Unknown Pleasures* (Ren xiao yao, 2002) is meant to contrast the boredom of everyday life in a small town with the yearning for excitement of its youth, his more recent reference to *Pulp Fiction* in *A Touch of Sin* (Tian zhuding, 2013) helps to vent frustration built up in this daily life.[7] Tarantino has been Jia's pal in his noir observation of Chinese life.

Whereas *Pulp Fiction*'s popularity in China is not related to any particular Chinese film, *Crazy Stone* has to take credit for Guy Ritchie's popularity in China. Ritchie's debut film *Lock, Stock and Two Smoking Barrels* is a crime comedy featuring a multi-plot-line heist story, noted for the pace and energy achieved in MTV pyrotechnics, and a resemblance to Tarantino hip gangster formula. Obviously, *Crazy Stone* owes a big debt in these aspects to this film. Stylistically, *Crazy Stone* appears to be a point-to-point parody of *Lock, Stock and Two Smoking Barrels* that many Chinese would just call copying. Ritchie's unique camera movement for the sake of intensity and violence of action inspired Ning Hao to feature his moving camera in his peculiar style of *ku, xuan,* and *che* (cool, showy and outlandish). Ritchie's multi-story-line narrative led Ning Hao not only to do the same but also heeded more to the narrative suspense and connection of his stories. Ritchie's linguistic mannerism in characterization ushered in Ning Hao's humorous characterization of folks of the grassroots, distinguished by effective use of Chinese dialects. Ritchie's heavy metal rock music encouraged Nin Hao to be mischievous with his own sound track, using traditional opera melody for modern chasing or featuring *Swan Lake* ballet melody played in style of rock and roll.

Before *Crazy Stone's* release (in 2006), Ritchie's 1998 film received limited attention in China, with only one article devoted to it, written by a graduate student of Beijing Film Academy who happened to have London connections. It discusses *Lock, Stock and Two Smoking Barrels* in relation to postmodernism, and it refers to Guy Ritchie as "the British Tarantino" (Wang Ying 2004, 51). Since 2006, the number of articles on Ritchie has mushroomed. The reason that *Crazy Stone* could magnify Ritchie's impact is that it has what Desser calls "an impulse toward cinephilia" (2003, 528) (related with an "intertextual chain of references, borrowings, and re-workings"), or what Naremore (2008, 196) calls the characteristics of parody, pastiche, and "plagiarism" from contemporary "image-bank" and the available "'nexus of fashion' that constitutes the popular conception of film noir," or what the Chinese popular culture calls an indulgence in "egao" (mischievous parody). Through its popularity, this characteristic of *Crazy Stone* has helped illustrate the hybrid taste of the Chinese audience in film consumption, sustained by an unregulated but flourishing video market. The parodies make the audience smile. "Egao," nonetheless, also promotes Chinese discussion of postmodernism, thus allowing the *Crazy Stone*-generated discourse to bridge popular culture and intellectual high culture in China.

4   MODERNITY: MODERNISM, POSTMODERNISM, AND POST-SOCIALISM

To situate 2006 carnival into the context of how the borrowed terms of modernism and postmodernism were used in post-Mao China, there is an uncanny sense that this black carnival occurred in China just as Harvard scholar Daniel Bell described the use of these terms in the Western context. In writing about the cultural contradictions of capitalism, Bell believes that modernism contains a contradiction of rationality (the basic requirement of the capitalist system) versus an ever greater emphasis on such values as feeling, personal gratification, and the total fulfillment of the self. To align with the latter, modernism constantly renews itself to maintain in the forefront (the *avant-garde*), in the name of advancing consciousness, to provide "renewed and sustained attacks on the social structure" (Bell 1976, 46). Craziness/madness, the counterpart of rationality, in this light, is very much called for,

> What is singular about this "tradition of the new" is that it allows art to be unfettered, to break down all genres and to explore all modes of experiences and sensation. Fantasy today has few costs other than the risk of individual madness. And even madness, in the writings of such social theorists as Michel Foucault and R. D. Laing, is now conceived to be a superior form of truth! (Bell 1976, 34)

Postmodernism, according to Bell, involves transformation from being "esoteric" to being an "ideology," from "avant-garde" to retreating to the "boredom with the old and the new," from a "gnostic mode" to a "widespread cultural movement," and from the effort of "aristocracy of the spirit" to that of "the mass" (Bell 1976, 52–53). When all this occurs, personal madness must converge to become a carnival so as to be in accordance with the postmodern temper, which, according to Bell, provides the psychological spearhead for an onslaught on the values and motivational patterns of the "ordinary" behavior, in the name of liberation, eroticism, freedom of impulse, and the like. (Bell 1976, 52)

This temper ushers in an age of "pop hedonism," in which "a bohemian life-style once limited to a tiny elite is now acted out on the giant screen of the mass media" (Bell 1976, 54).

In China, this particular modernism that Bell has described merged with the post-Mao need for rediscovering human nature, which for decades had been employed simplistically according to political agendas. In the 1980s, Chinese modernism flourished in all sorts of *avant-garde*, formalistic experiments in film, literature, and art. The tension contained in the term, inhibitions, and restraints versus impulses and feelings resonated so well with Chinese cultural needs of the period. This particular modernism becomes the context for the crazy-titled films of the late 1980s that we identified earlier. Postmodernism soon followed, particularly since the 1990s. Postmodernism, according to Xudong Zhang's in-depth study, "entered China via the intellectuals who seek theoretical inspirations from, and discursive synchronization with, the West, and which is largely limited to small circles of literary and art criticism" (2008, 136). Yet, this kind of postmodernism in China was held responsible for the rise of a new kind of mass culture, distinctively playful, that may well be called "pop hedonism." A "Hedonist Manifesto" in a Chinese newspaper in 2003, clearly a pastiche of the "Communist Manifesto," declared that "we claim to be hedonists … we don't want to hide our value orientation … we believe that pleasure is our purpose of life … to enjoy pleasure is our natural rights."[8] With enriched, liberated human nature functioning in every one of them, the Chinese mass and their seeking for happiness, including the frustration in the process, is a shared feeling since it is, as Bell described, constantly projected on the "giant screen of mass media." When *Crazy Stone*, created a black carnival in China via this giant screen in 2006, some Chinese theoreticians (Zheng Dongtian et al. 2006) used the phenomenon to confirm the need of postmodernism in accounting for it.

In the popular success of *Crazy Stone*, the film is highly praised for its "formalism," that is, its skillful blending of unusual camera angles, eruptive camera movement, and emotive rhythm of editing with an ironic mix of humor and violence, nonlinear but suspenseful multi-story lines, and a host of popular culture references. The film builds *egao* connections with many popular films, Chinese and foreign, circulating in the Chinese video market. Concern arises whether the success of this film is primarily based on copying *Pulp Fiction* (1994) and *Lock, Stock and Two Smoking Barrels* (1998). The copying, however, is tolerated by audiences in China. What leads the audience to overlook the similarities is what I would call "the Forrest Gump elements" (Kuoshu 2015, 7) in *Crazy Stone*, that is, its connection with the Chinese grassroots. Chinese online reviews appreciate how *Crazy Stone* Sinicized the foreign impact and how insightful comedies about lives of ordinary folks ensured the connection of the film with the majority of the audience. A review in *Nanfang dushi bao* (Southern Metropolitan Gazette) declared, "The value of *Crazy Stone* is that it is in touch with the pulse of the ordinary folks, which lends the film a solid foundation to build its own drama. The reality showcased in this film is what those established directors, who are becoming more middle class, élite and aloof from the masses, can hardly see."[9] This review reads surprisingly similar to an earlier Western review of *Pulp Fiction*, which believes that the film "shook up a tired, bloated movie industry and used a world of lively lowlifes to reflect how dull other movies had become" (Siskel and Ebert 1995). The copying and the tolerance to copying here, it turns out, is not just about film forms; the formalistic impact of *Pulp Fiction* and *Lock, Stock and Two Smoking Barrels* on *Crazy Stone* has brought with it a cultural dynamic for change and a revolt against the doldrums of the élite culture by drawing energy from the grassroots. *Egao* may very well be a Chinese term referring to an Asian cultural traffic, but the works produced in this trend, as *Crazy Stone* testifies, unavoidably have to incorporate Western elements in the culture of globalization.

In *egao*, the Forrest Gump elements call for both street reality (real-life experience) and virtual reality (film or style invoked reality) in audience response. In a new trendy film style, the Chinese audience feels better connected not only to their everyday reality but also to diversified, international human responses to similar situations through films. Here lies the social power of formalism. The connection is first of all that of the forms and then that of the resemblance to actual life situations. Just as *Pulp Fiction*'s style "is created from the context of movie life rather than real life" (Dancyger 2002, 228), Chinese *egao* films also first build connections with their stylistic predecessors. To tie the two levels of reality, the ideological orientations become unavoidable. In the postmodern/postsocialist playfulness of the Chinese *egao* trend, one can easily see how it tends to correspond with the Western discourse of postmodernism. Of *Pulp Fiction*, scholars from the West have commented on its "postmodern insouciance" (Kolker 2000, 281), and on it for "referencing of previous aesthetic forms and styles [that] moves beyond...empty pastiche, sustaining an 'inventive and affirmative' mode of postmodernism" (Constable 2004, 54). By copying and Sinicizing *Pulp Fiction*, *Crazy Stone* created its own insouciant collage and made it possible for the Chinese audience to understand a doubling of the street and the virtual realities in the name of postmodernism. The Chinese online encyclopedia defines the folk orientation of postmodernism (hou xiandai xing)—in reference to *Crazy Stone* and its Western stylistic predecessors—as "the popular culture of the masses," "the grassroots spirit," and "a deconstruction of the monolithic grand narrative."[10]

Postmodernism in China, however, is really an inflection of post-socialism. Surveying how recently scholarship "has produced a dazzling variety of contexts (aesthetic, industrial, political) in which the noir phenomenon might be approached," Jennifer Fay and Justus Nieland made an insightful argument about the global nature as well as the local inflection of film noir (Fay and Nieland 2010, 141):

> If noir can be thought of as a problem of the uncanniness of capitalist democracy (Sobchack), one encoded in the history of modernity's built environments (Dimendberg), or one marked by the traumatic returns of a submerged history of state violence (Rabinowitz), then this sensibility is also a global one, which is not to deny its local inflections. (Fay and Nieland 2010, 142)

These problems with political system, ideology, economic development, value, and environment may indeed confront humanities in any nation or culture. The timing, size, and urgency of these problems, however, are bound to be different from nation to nation. In China, the country's totalitarian political past and its contemporary post-socialist adjustment unavoidably are going to contextualize the Chinese neo-noir films and decide the nature of these films' "traumatic returns." To maintain their critical edges, these films need to remain to be B films, that is, not those produced by mainstream studio systems but those more related to independent filmmaking and subcultures. In the recent fad of noir comedy in China, Chinese film artists and critics have already started to worry if they can successfully maintain the B status of their films so that these films can remain to be noir. Sha Dan, for example, observed that although noir comedies in China should be considered subculture, "they are being incorporated into the mainstream in the contexts of the reigning ideological indoctrination and rising consumerism" (Sha Dan 2009, 70). Sha Dan was concerned that the incorporation was already making the noir films less noir but he was also hopeful that film artists have creative ability to deal with the process of incorporation to remain to be the noir critics. From two remarks made by Ning Hao, the director of *Crazy Stone*, we detect some strategies adopted by these artists. Ning Hao keeps aloof from ideological indoctrination: "I only care that my film is great to watch. I grew up being preached to and hated most the preaching kind of education. I want to embody education in fun; I present absurdity—not intending to criticize or educate anyone" (quoted in Sha Dan 2009, 70). Ning Hao justifies his noir comedies with the need of the audience and the implied effect of social stability, which has been a prominent ideological goal in China: "Where does the humor come from? Laughter is a critique, a way to live, and a release through critique. The more comedies the audience watch, the more released they become. They thus have a good mood in life" (quoted in Sha Dan 2009, 67).

5   Laughter: Carnival Revelry and Darkness

So that a cycle of *Crazy Stone* initiated films be considered neo-noir, however, one has to consider if a carnival revelry shared by most of these films may defeat the sense of darkness that is essential to film noir, traditional or neo. After all, most of these Chinese films are comedies that frequently become dark rather than dark films that become funny occasionally.

(1) Generally speaking, laughter was unwanted in the traditional noir films of 1940s and 1950s. However, since these films then were informed by existentialism and surrealism, they actually had potential to illicit chilled laughter. "If the surrealists saw the Hollywood thriller as a theater of cruelty," Naremore observes, "the existentialists saw it as an absurdist novel" (Naremore 95–96, 20). It is not unlikely for absurdity to illicit laughter.

(2) In addition, the formal elements of film noir needed to change in different contexts. In its genre history, as Naremore noticed, "film noir was also a prisoner of conventions. ...in the 1940s, films about crime and gangs possessed a bizarre quality reminiscent of the surrealists of Kafka; by the 1950s, however, social criticism was smothered by banal plot conventions, and 'incoherence' became

predictable" (Naremore 95–96, 19–20). In today's postmodern/ post-socialist context, such elements like pastiche and trickery decide that neo-noir often needs to be mischievously dark. "Neo noirs," Hibbs deliberates, "almost inevitably draw attention to their style, going so far in some cases as to make style itself the subject of the film. In the very act of recognizing the artifice, we are in on the joke, on the sleight of hand performed by the film-maker. The result is amusement, even laughter" (Conard 2007, 138). For Winfried Fluck, neo-noir also appears "playful" since it is "a cinema without depth, so that self-dissolution becomes pleasurable entertainment" (Fluck 2001, 405).

(3) The post-war, French-initiated film noir discourse also showed a tendency of focusing heavily on the ideological positions of the films, allowing a wide range of forms to be used by these films to work against those used in the films of the mainstream culture. In this discursive tradition, as Naremore observes, "noir is not simply a descriptive term, but the name for a critical tendency within the popular cinema—an anti-genre that reveals the dark side of savage capitalism" (Naremore 95–96, 20). In our case, comic as they are, if our Chinese films fall into "an anti-genre" artistically and ideologically, they tend to become dark in producing the senses of disorientation, disillusion, and alienation.

In deliberating a similar problem of the role of laughter in noir films, Greg Tuck encounters some difficulty of fitting Quentin Tarantino's films properly within his elaborate approaches such as comic being plural (unfinalized, disseminative, dependent on context and the intertextuality of creator, text, and contemplator); comedy functioning according to superiority, relief, and incongruity theories; surrealism's antipathy toward sentiment allowing comedy to work in noir films; comedy being needed in grotesque realism to produce a sense of darkness; and so on. "Tarantino's films," Tuck deliberates, "are often structured around deeply sentimental attachments" and for that reason, he found Tarantino films "simply not dark" (Tuck 2009, 165, 166). This difficulty and Tarantino's popularity in the noir world forces Tuck to reconsider the implication of "neo" in the term of neo-noir. Tuck deliberates,

> Maybe we have misled ourselves by applying the term "neo" to Tarantino in the first place and his films are not "neo" in the sense that the prefix suggests

a continuation, revival, homage or even a remediation. Noir is not regenerated by Tarantino's mode of pastiche, but consumed and negated. What his films offer us, therefore, is a post-noir world where we no longer laugh at the dark and nor are we afraid of it. We have simply been anaesthetized against it. (Tuck 2009, 166)

The idea that a film in reference to film noir may consume and negate the sense of darkness in itself but it should still be considered part of the noir world (call it post-noir if you wish) is actually important for my argument of considering dark comedies inspired by *Crazy Stone* as an episode of the global neo-noir. The Chinese episode owes a lot to the impact of Tarantino. It is situated in a general discourse of postmodernism, particularly emphasizing intertextuality and the use of pastiche as fashioned by the Chinese mischievous trend of *egao*. In the general revelry of a cultural carnival, darkness conveyed in some of the Chinese films, sustains societal, cultural, or ideological critiques. In the meantime, this darkness is also a commodity for popular entertainment, an aid for laughter, and a fashion of stylistic borrowing. Some of these films may not be fundamentally dark but they tend to refer to other noir films or use noir elements.

6   Nihilism, Cynicism, and Chinese Neo-noir

The discussion of nihilism is an essential element of film noir scholarship. Filmic nihilism in relation to modernity refers primarily to Nietzsche's use of this concept. Earlier in tracing the implications of craziness, we encountered Nietzsche's madman and this madman's need for a theater. Now we must emphasize that Nietzsche's madman functions as his Dionysian character for the performance of nihilism. In a metaphorical sense, our carnival of 2006 may also be seen as a Dionysian revelry in which darkness is produced by clowning. The resulting vision may often resemble what Jack Nicholson's Joker showcases in the 1989 film *Batman,* but in Chinese films it is the petty thieves, small-time gangsters, corrupted officials, tainted businessmen, or any misguided characters involved in a de-centered clowning, who portray a dark world.

In Chinese scholarship, nihilism is often discussed in relation to modernity. Wang Zhihong and Zhu Shiqun (2012, 25–26) identify a four-stage development of nihilism in China as the Chinese response to modernity's knock on the door. (1) In the May Fourth Era of the 1910s, the new cultural movement denounced Chinese traditional culture in a nihilistic fashion. (2) As an aftermath of the Cultural Revolution (1966–1976), nihilism shows in total disillusion with the country's political values and system. (3) The collapse of the Soviet Union deepened the Chinese popular mistrust in the value and social systems built according to Marxist ideology. (4) With market forces and commercialism becoming dominant in China, nihilism emerges in the process when "technical rationality deconstructs human-value rationality" and in "the specter of materialistic desires functioning as values."

While this chronology is helpful in identifying moments of crisis in Chinese beliefs, one also wonders if it is appropriate to call this kind of crisis nihilism. After all, recent Chinese history has left very little room for the development of individualist subjectivity and humanism in relation to it. "In modern China," scholar Yuan Zushe points out, "in the enlightenment cloaked in names of 'science' and 'progress,' individuals are not the objects of but the tools for the enlightenment" (2009, 7). Yuan believes that the Chinese feelings of anxiety, emptiness, and meaninglessness are often caused by "the lack of realms for self-experiencing practice for the subjectivity in the modern sense" (2009, 7). Considering China's lack of religious culture (like Christianity that Nietzsche finds Western culture has outgrown) and its lack of modernist, individualist culture (shown in a self who can use nihilism as a moment of the deepest self-reflection of humanity and thus master crisis), one tends to agree with Yuan that China has not stepped across the threshold into Western nihilism in the strict philosophical and cultural sense. In most cases, the use of nihilism in recent Chinese discourse remains an analogy about superficial similarities between China and the West in having crises of values and beliefs. When nihilism is applied to the discussion of contemporary Chinese mass culture, it also causes anxiety among scholars. He Lei, for example, worries that in post-Mao China, from Wang Shuo's hooliganism to the more recent *egao* trends, negative nihilism has persisted with China's youth culture and mass culture for too long without showing enough signs of positive nihilism. Scholars have also coined "silly-laughter-ism" (shaxiao zhuyi), initiating from Tao Dongfeng's discussion of the phenomenon, to refer to the negative nihilist tendency in Chinese popular entertainment.

For a more productive perspective to access the cultural implication of our 2006 carnival, I believe that we need to become more attentive to a related concept, cynicism, the Chinese translation of which is literally "dog Confucianism" (quan ru zhuyi). Whereas the "dog" part of the translation retains the Greek etymology of the term plus legends about the founders of ancient cynicism, the "Confucianism" part of the term suggests that in ancient China, where mainstream culture relied on such worldly ideals as "an enlightened emperor aided by sage administers" (*ming jun xian xiang*) and a "perfect self-cultivation combined with benevolent governance" ("being sage inside and being kingly outside"/ *nei sheng wai wang*) to inspire its people, there is plenty room for cynicism.

Michel Foucault draws our attention to the canonical characteristics of how dog images are associated with ancient Cynics: "unconcealed, independent, straight, sovereign life." The dog-like life of ancient Cynics, to him, is a demonstration of "true life" though it takes it "to the point of its extreme consequence and reversal" (2012, 243). The four dog characteristics, for example, are all given forms of drama: unconcealed life is dramatized in "the practice of nakedness and shameless," independent life in "the form of poverty," straight life in "the form of animality," and sovereign life in the form of "the militant life" of battle and struggle (2012, 283). What ancient Cynics did, as I commented about Nietzsche's madman earlier, is to maintain a theater of shocks, only this time it is more like a pantomime that relies heavily on acting rather than on words. In other words, Cynics preferred life (styles, aesthetics, and mode of life) to doctrine and used their way of life to undermine certain doctrines. Here is how Foucault describes it:

> The forms and habits which usually stamp existence and give it its features must be replaced by the effigy of the principles traditionally accepted by philosophy. But the very fact of applying these principles to life itself, rather than merely maintaining them in the element of the *logos*, by the fact that they give a form to life ... [which] reveals other lives, the lives of others. (2012, 244)

The most important of Foucault's ideas to our discussion is that the Cynics' way of "constituting the body itself as the visible theater" (2012, 183) is not the hindrance to truth but a way to truth, even though this theater can often be eruptive, violent, and scandalous. Satire, comedy, and carnivalesque practices, Foucault believes, are the "privileged site" for Cynic expression (186–87). This theater is "banal" and it is "on the fringe of institutions, laws, and recognized social groups" but it has its universal appeal (2012, 201). The theme Foucault wants to establish for this kind of Cynic expression in Western history is that it is "life as scandal of the truth" or "style of life as site of emergence of the truth" (2012, 180). In a more fundamental way, Foucault makes the Cynic mode of expression and being an important aspect of Western philosophy in the Socratic tradition of posing the question of an *other* life as contrasted to the Platonic question of the other world. The traditional Chinese worldview tends to associate more easily with the *other*-life philosophy. Using this perspective to think again of the Chinese etymological metaphor of the character *kuang* (craziness) as dogs challenging the king, the Cynic element of *kuang* as a performed mode of being becomes rather revealing.

A difficulty that keeps us from using Foucault's insight about cynicism to explain the implications of the 2006 carnival is the prevailing idea in China that modern cynicism almost has nothing to do with ancient cynicism. "Compared with ancient cynicism," scholar Xu Ben points out, "the most important characteristics of the contemporary cynicism is that it has changed into a nihilism and do-nothing-ism that has cast aside ethic principles and the conscience" (2014, 33). An anonymous writer of the entry of "contemporary cynicism" of Chinese online encyclopedia *Baidu baike* describes this difference as that between *fen shi ji su* (be angry with society and be picky with the customs) and *wan shi bu gong* (to play with the world with no respect).[11] The former is the depiction of ancient cynicism and the latter is that of contemporary cynicism, which the entry defines as a complete nihilism. Some aphorisms concerning contemporary cynicism collected by the entry helps us get some perspective on general negative feeling about the concept: with an abundance of worldly wisdom but no passion for justice, one becomes a cynic; a cynic knows virtue without praising it and knows evil but chooses not to denounce it; absolute political power corrupts, and absolute lack of power in politics also corrupts, since both lead others to believe that power is everything; totalitarianism turns people into cynics and these cynics believe that they are the only ones who understand totalitarianism inside out. Inspecting these aphorisms, one can't help notice the prominence of the impact of totalitarianism and its role in the making of contemporary Chinese cynicism. The difficulty we have here is both unique and not so unique. The uniqueness has to do with its Chinese specificity which incorporates Chinese ancient cultural traditions, ancient totalitarianism, and the recent cultural impact of political totalitarianism. The uniqueness also has to do with the much stronger degree of moral anxiety caused by contemporary cynicism. The general attitude change that is based on, as Foucault puts it, a "contrast of Cynicism with a rather positive value, ancient Cynicism, and a cynicism with a rather negative value, modern cynicism" is a widely shared feeling, East and West (2012, 180).

Foucault was not so enthusiastic about this contrast between capitalized and small-case cynicism, not only because "there was considerable ambiguity in the way in which ancient culture regarded and perceived Cynicism," but also because of the need to historicize cynicism of "diverse forms, different practices, and styles of existence modeled according to different schemas" (2012, 180). From the four German books on this subject that Foucault surveyed,[12] the connection between ancient and contemporary cynicism is also not seen as a total discontinuity; the idea of self-assertion, for example, is seen as common to both ancient and contemporary cynicism—"this self-assertion does not take place by reference to animality, but is effectuated in the face of and in relation to absurdity and the universal absence of meaning" (2012, 179).

Based on the studies of one of these books, Peter Sloterdijk's *Critique of Cynical Reason*, Slovenian theorist Slavoj Zizek offers us a particularly pertinent insight on the role of cynicism in the totalitarian society. Zizek distinguishes *kynicism* (capitalized cynicism) from cynicism,

> Kynicism represents the popular, plebeian rejection of the official culture by means of irony and sarcasm: the classical kynical procedure is to confront the pathetic phrases of the ruling official ideology—its solemn, grave tonality—with everyday banality and to hold them up to ridicule, thus exposing behind the sublime *noblesse* of the ideological phrases the egotistical interests, the violence, the brutal claims to power. (1989, 29)

This cultural stance, Zizek believes, is more pragmatic than argumentative, that is, as popular subversion, it is often a moment-by-moment and incident-by-incident response to the mainstream ideology rather than a theory. In a way, kynicism may still remind people of ancient cynicism, ancient cynic use of body as theater, and such themes as cynicism as *other* life or cynic mode of being and expression as scandal of the truth. Confronted with this particular kynicism, lower-case cynicism can be detected in the ruling culture,

> It recognizes, it takes into account, the particular interest behind the ideological universality, the distance between the ideological mask and the reality, but it still finds reasons to retain the mask. (Zizek 1989, 29)

Instead of morally denouncing the cynicism contained in today's totalitarian ideology (which he can't refrain from doing), Zizek believes that cynicism is part of the mechanism of his understanding of ideology, which is a Lacanian unconscious process containing a series of justifications (such as various cynic assumptions) and spontaneous socio-symbolic rituals. Zizek's perspective allows us the opportunity to approach both capitalized and lower-case cynicism in the 2006 carnival either as current Chinese ideological components or as symptoms, shown as the ideology's illusion, deviation, or rejection.

Crazy Stone, which showcases a widespread sense of defeat among contemporary Chinese, can serve as an example here. If one calls this film's depiction of contemporary Chinese life cynical, according to Li Shengtao, it is because the film denounces the myth of the government-engineered modernization agenda that produced the new rich and glorified wealth: "new life styles showcase lives of the new rich to the masses, using fantastic but out-of-reach myths both to provoke the desire of the masses and to feed their wishful thinking for wealth and social status. This ideology has caught the masses between fanciful thinking and awkwardness" (2007, 52). The filmic protest offered by *Crazy Stone* and the ideological critique contained in *Crazy Stone* discourse, using Zizek's framework, should be categorized as a *kynic* expression. In addition, although many are well aware of the awkwardness showcased by the film, they choose to justify the need for an ideology that promotes modernization and individual prosperity. Cynicism was initially shown in the 1990s in what is known as an under-the-table deal of "shut up and get rich," a strategy using cynicism to tame political dissidents and to lessen political crisis. While the promotion of individual wealth will leave many essential social and cultural problems un-addressed, people are willing to accept enough justification contained in this myth for them, to use Zizek's phrase, to "retain the mask." The list of justifications may go on and on and may change from time to time. These justifications may include economic development, social stability, common welfare, national pride, or national defense. Such cynic justifications are essential components of this ideology in today's China.

In making the argument that a cycle of *Crazy Stone* initiated films constitute an episode of global neo-noir, among the various implications of the term, I am thinking of it more as a cultural phenomenon that connects filmmakers, film critics, and film audiences rather than an industrial genre; more as a film-initiated style circulated in the celluloid world than a way of depicting street reality; more as a formula to boost film consumption than an *auteur* effort to enrich film art; and more as a bridge that connects popular entertainment and the high culture's rational interpretations than a rather isolated marginal subculture. Sha Dan, a Chinese critic, offered a similar approach in suggesting, in a practical manner, that the noir features in recent Chinese films are not constituting a genre but testifying to a cultural mode (2009, 68). In this way, noir may combine with and show up in such genres as road films, screwball comedies, and crime thrillers. The argument that a cycle of films inspired by *Crazy Stone* constitutes an episode of global neo-noir is meant more to open up channels of discursive, celluloid, and aesthetic connections so as to enrich our understanding of the phenomenon than to categorize films into a new genre.

Since some topics I discuss in the following chapters are not visible in the table of contents, I would like to point them out here. Chapter 2 explores craziness and noir in a differed discursive context well over a decade prior to the emergence of the stone phenomenon. A discussion of Chinese fascination with Herbert Marcuse and Milan Kundera in the 1980s helps highlight the era's interests in human nature and the related cultural concerns. Known under the umbrella term of *rehumanization*, these concerns inform my discussion of three crazy-titled, dark films. They also inform my exploration for a reason for the accidental, stylistic similarity of these films with traditional, American film noir. Much had changed between the 1980s and the emergence of the stone phenomenon in 2006, discursively known as a change from the modern to the postmodern in Chinese terms. Chapter 3 offers a road map to the changed alignment of discourses, using such hot terms of the stone phenomenon as carnival, grassroots, and *egao* as points of departure for a survey. What of interest is how the concept of *hou xiaozi* (post petty bourgeois) revises the traditional social concept of the masses, which enriches the meanings of the grassroots, and how Chinese subcultural trends of Generation *Ku*, *Xiaozi* (petty bourgeois), Generation *Q*, and *wulitou* (not seeing where it's coming from) rejuvenate the rebel flair of the grassroots. The Chinese scholarly access of *egao* lends us a glimpse of the resourcefulness of the Chinese scholars when they give this concept a postmodern spin. *Egao* is understood in light of Derrida's deconstruction of "grand logocentrism," Stjepan Gabriel Meštrović's post-emotionalism, as well as Tiphane Samoyault's intertextuality. Chapter 4 selects a handful of films inspired by *Crazy Stone* in production to help understand not only the various aspects of a neo-noir episode of Chinese filmmaking but also its marketing. Here, the joining of hands of *Crazy Stone* with another dark-horse film that emerged in the same year of 2006, *My Own Swordsman*, formulates an interesting networking of influences. To wrap this mini book up and to highlight the monkey imagery produced in a film movement initiated by *Crazy Stone*, Chap. 5 reflects on cinematic craziness by discussing Huang Bo's mini film *Crazy Twins* and Ning Hao's third title of his crazy trilogy, *Crazy Alien*.

NOTES

1. At the time of its release, *The Curse of the Golden Flowers* claims to have surpassed Chen Kaige's *The Promise* to become the most expensive Chinese film to date. The plot of the film is based on Cao Yu's 1934 play *Thunderstorm*. Feng Xiaogang's *The Banquet* is allegedly an adaption of William Shakespeare's *Hamlet*. A prominent event in 2005 that started the Chinese popular trend of mischievous parody was the uploading of He Ge's "*Yige mantou yinfa de xuean*" ("A bloody case all caused by a bun"), a short video to mock Chen Kaige's film *The Promise* (Wuji, 2005). The video triggered off heated responses and a whirlwind of downloading.

2. Xinzhao Cultural Transmission Center, the producer of *Crazy Necklace*, issued a sixteen-page PowerPoint document to explain the market potential of the film (accessed Sept. 11, 2015, at http://wenku.baidu.com/view/142a05360b4c2e3f57276333.html). It claims that *Crazy Stone* has helped increase the box office income of Chinese films and the year 2009 witnesses a 40 percent rise in income compared with 2008. It assures the investors that the increase will continue in 2010 to guarantee their investment. It claims that they can maintain "the myth of craziness" without the presence of Ning Hao, and they invite investors "to have a journey along with craziness."

3. See *The Analects of Confucius*, 13.21. The translation is mine.

4. See Zhuangzi's chapter of "Mountain Woods." The translation is mine.

5. See Silbergeld (2004). In an earlier book, I wrote the following comment concerning this topic: "I would suggest that the genre that *Vertigo* belongs to, *film noir*, offers clues to further understand this coincidental resemblance of Lou's film to an earlier masterpiece. As we know, among the fountainheads of the classic period American film noir is Italian neo-realism, a cinematic tradition that graduates of Beijing Film Academy tend to admire. Problem pictures and semi-documentary crime thrillers influenced by Italian neo-realism in the post-War America led to the formation of a cinematic mood of cynicism, darkness and despair, which in turn pro-

duced more crime films and melodramas about an urban jungle of crime and corruption" (Kuoshu 2011, 152).

6. In this review, Scott Foundas writes, "The spirits of Raymond Chandler and James M. Cain course through *Black Coal, Thin Ice*, a bleak but powerful, carefully controlled detective thriller in which—as with all the best noirs—there are no real heroes or villains, only various states of compromise." This passage shows up as a citation for a Chinese review of the film in terms of *film noir* (Zou Ping 2015).

7. Jia's pastiche of *Pulp Fiction* has been widely discussed by reviewers. In *A Touch of Sin*, an embittered miner, Da Hai, hides in the mine owner's Maserati, where the owner discovers him and tries to buy him off. The next image is Da Hai's blood-spattered face in the back seat—as in the famous scene in *Pulp Fiction*.

8. See *Yangcheng wanbao, xinwen zhoukan* (*Guangzhou Evening Gazette*) issue 314, 2003. Quoted in He Lei (2015, 148).

9. Quoted in the *Baidu baike* (Chinese online encyclopedia) entry for *Crazy Stone*. Accessed January 20, 2012. http://baike.baidu.com/view/307172.htm

10. *Baidu baike* (Chinese online encyclopedia) entry for Guy Ritchie. Accessed January 20, 2012. http://baike.baidu.com/view/375209.htm

11. The data of a Chinese web dictionary shows that in most cases these two Chinese phrases, with no distinction, are just directly translated as "cynicism" or to be "cynical."

12. See Foucault (2012) for the authors and titles of these books. At the time when Foucault delivered his lecture, he had not read the fourth book, which, in English translation, is Peter Sloterdijk's *Critique of Cynical Reason* (London: Verso, 1988). This fourth book is Slavoj Zizek's reference in developing his theory on cynicism in totalitarian ideology.

REFERENCES

CHINESE LANGUAGE SOURCES

Chen Hongxiu. 2012. Heise youmo yu zhongguo dalu xiju dianying: jianlun heise youmo pian yu heise xiju pian de yitong (Black Humor Films and Chinese Mainland Comic Films: Also on the Difference Between Black Humor and Dark Comedy Films). *Qinghai shehui kexue* (Qinghai Journal of Social Sciences) 2: 177–180.

Hao Jian. 2002. Xushi kuanghuan he guaixiao de heise: haolaiwu guaicai kunting talandino chuangzuo lun (The Carnival Narration and the Darkness of Bizarre Laughter: On Film Arts of Hollywood Weird Genius Quentin Tarantino). *Dangdai dianying* (Contemporary Cinema) 1: 59–68.

He Lei. 2015. Lun dangdai zhongguo dazhong wenhua jiazhi xuwuzhuyi de qux-iang lujing (On Orientations of Value Nihilism in Today's Chinese Mass Culture). *Dangdai wentan* (Contemporary Literary Platform) 3: 146–150.

Li Shengtao. 2007. 'Fengkuang de shitou' daodi fanfeng le shenme? (What Does *Crazy Stone* Jeer at After All?). *Dianying pingjie* (Movie Review) 12: 51–52.

Meng Fanxuan. 2014. Bairi yanhuo: zhongguo heise dianying tansuo daolu de shuguang (Black Coal, Thin Ice: The Dawn of China's Research of Film Noir). *Jin Tian* (Golden Field) 299: 123–124.

Sha Dan. 2009. Xiofei huangdan: wanjin zhongguo hese xiju de moshi yu bianxi (To Consume Absurdity: Analyzing the Modes of Recent Black Comedy). *Dianying yishu* (Film Arts) 6: 67–71.

Wang Ying. 2004. Hou xiandai fenwei xia de lundun gushi (London Story in Postmodern Aura). *Beijing dianying xueyuan xuebao* (Journal of Beijing Film Academy) 5: 51–56.

Wang Zhihong, and Zhu Shiqun. 2012. Dui zhongguo dangdai xuwuzhuyi sichao de zhexue sikao (A Philosophical Consideration of Contemporary Trends of Nihilism in China). *Hebei xuekan* (Hebei Academic Journal) 32 (2): 25–30.

Wu Guanping, et al. 2006. *Fengkuang de shitou*: hese de kuanghuan (*Crazy Stone*: Dark Carnival). *Dianying yishu* (Film Arts) 5: 73–75.

Xi Yongfeng. 2006. Fengkuang de shitou: heise youmo yu kunhuo rensheng (*Crazy Stone*: Black Humor and Puzzling Life). *Dianying wenxue* (Film Literature) 10: 3–6.

Xiu Ti. 2005. Dangdai zhongguo dianying zhong de heise youmo (Black Humor in Contemporary Chinese Film). *Dianying yishu* (Film Arts) 1: 118–121

Xu Ben. 2014. Dangdai quanruzhuyi de liangxin yu xiwang (Conscience and Hope in Contemporary Cynicism). *Dushu* (Book Review) 7: 29–37.

Ye Shuxian. 1999. Zhongguo wenhua zhong de fengkuang (Madness in Chinese Culture). *Xin dongfang* (New East) 1: 40–54.

Yu Yingshi. 1987. *Shi yu zhongguo wenhua* (Shi Scholar and Chinese Culture). Shanghai renmin chubanshe.

Yuan Zushe. 2009. *Fengkuang de daijia* bitan (Cultural Mirror of Nihilism and Practical Dilemma of Chinese "Self-Experience"). *Shaanxi shifan daxue xuebao* (Journal of Shaanxi Normal University, Philosophy and Social Sciences Edition) 6: 5–11.

Zheng Dongtian, et al. 2006. Xinzuo pingyi: *fengkuang de shitou* (Discussion of New Movies: On *Crazy Stone*). *Dangdai dianying* (Contemporary Cinema) 5: 15–20.

Zou Ping. 2015. Lun dianying *bairi yanhuo* de heise xing he xin tansuo (On the Darkness and New Orientations in the Film *Black Coal, Thin Ice*). *Zhongguo dianying pinglun* (Chinese Movie Review) 17: 24–26.

ENGLISH LANGUAGE SOURCES

Appadurai, Arjun. 1996. *Modernity at Large: Cultural Dimensions of Globalization*. Minneapolis: University of Minnesota Press.

Bell, Daniel. 1976. *The Cultural Contradictions of Capitalism*. New York: Basic Books.

Bussanich, John, and Nicholas D. Smith, eds. 2013. *The Bloomsbury Companion to Socrates*. London/New Delhi/New York/Sydney: Bloomsbury.

Conard, Mark T., ed. 2007. *The Philosophy of Neo-Noir*. Kentucky: The University Press of Kentucky.

Constable, Catherine. 2004. Postmodernism and Film. In *The Cambridge Companion to Postmodernism*, ed. Steven Connor, 43–61. Cambridge: Cambridge University Press.

Dancyger, Ken. 2002. *The Technique of Film and Video Editing: History, Theory, and Practice*. 3rd ed. New York: Focal Press.

Desser, David. 2003. Global Noir: Genre Film in the Age of Transnationalism. In *Film Genre Reader III*, ed. Barry Keith Grant, 516–536. Austin: University of Texas Press.

Farber, Stephen. 1974. Movie Crazy. *The Hudson Review* 27 (2): 252–258.

Fay, Jennifer, and Justus Nieland. 2010. *Film Noir: Hard-Boiled Modernity and Cultures of Globalization*. London/New York: Routledge.

Fluck, Winfried. 2001. Crime, Guilt, and Subjectivity in *Film Noir*. *Amerikastudien/American Studies* 46 (3): 379–408.

Foucault, Michel. 2012. *The Courage of Truth: The Government of Self and Others II*. New York: Picador, Palgrave Macmillan.

Foundas, Scott. 2014. Film Review: *Black Coal, Thin Ice*. Posted February 13, 2014. https://variety.com/2014/film/reviews/berlin-film-review-black-coal-thin-ice-1201099676/. Accessed 15 Aug 2019.

Fusso, Susanne. 1994. *Essays on Gogol: Logos and the Russian Word*. Chicago: Northwestern University Press.

Kolker, Robert. 2000. *A Cinema of Loneliness: Penn, Stone, Kubrick, Scorsese, Spielberg, Altman*. 3rd ed. New York: Oxford University Press.

Kuoshu, Harry. 2011. *Metro Movies: Cinematic Urbanism in Post-Mao China*. Carbondale/Edwardsville: Southern Illinois University Press.

———. 2015. Forrest Gump Becomes a Chinese Film Director: Idealism, Formalism, and an In-between Audience. *Global Studies Journal* 8 (1): 1–11.

Lu Xun. 1977. *Selected Stories of Lu Hsun*. New York/London: Norton & Company.

Naremore, James. 1995–1996. American Film Noir: The History of an Idea. *Film Quarterly* 49 (2): 12–28.

———. 2008. *More Than Night: Film Noir in Its Contexts*. Updated and Expanded Edition. Berkeley: University of California Press.

Silbergeld, Jerome. 2004. *Hitchcock with a Chinese Face: Cinematic Doubles, Oedipal Triangles, and China's Moral Voice.* Seattle: University of Washington Press.

Siskel, Gene, and Roger Ebert. 1995. Pulp Faction: The Tarantino Generation. *Pulp Fiction* DVD. Burbank: Buena Vista Home Entertainment.

Tuck, Greg. 2009. Laughter in the Dark: Irony, Black Comedy and Noir in the Films of David Lynch, the Coen Brothers and Quentin Tarantino. In *Neo-Noir*, ed. Mark Bould et al., 152–167. London/New York: Wallflower Press.

Zhang, Xudong. 2008. *Postsocialism and Cultural Politics: China in the Last Decade of the Twentieth Century.* Durham/London: Duke University Press.

Zhou, Zuyan. 1994. Carnivalization in *The Journey to the West*: Cultural Dialogism in Fictional Festivity. *Chinese Literature: Essays, Articles, Reviews (CLEAR)* 16: 69–92.

Zizek, Slavoj. 1989. *The Sublime Object of Ideology.* London/New York: Verso.

CHAPTER 2

Prelude: *Rehumanization* Craziness and Traditional Noir

Abstract Contrasting the *Crazy Stone* phenomenon of 2006, the cultural craziness showcased in the 1980s had a different era feel. Instead of sarcastic indulgence in cheers and jeers, instead of joking parodies bouncing in the wide expanse of either the cyber-connected world or what Desser calls "cinephilia" (the intertextual chain of filmic references, borrowings, and re-workings), and instead of a carnival revelry, the craziness showcased then was more like a morbid reaction induced by political traumas, a pubescent confusion of growing up in a cultural closure, and a hesitant rendezvous with craziness as a path to enrichment coupled with a fear of the doom it may bring. This chapter discusses three crazy-titled films of the 1980s to explore their connection with the current neo-noir episode of Chinese cinema. The contemporary call for *rehumanization*, the meaning of modernism then, the impact of Herbert Marcuse and Milan Kundera, and these films' resemblance to traditional film noir are investigated to inform the discussion.

Keywords Craziness • *Rehumanization* • Modernism • Eros • Herbert Marcuse • Milan Kundera • Zhou Xiaowen

1   "MODERNIST" CRAZINESS

Three crazy-titled films, Liu Guoquan's *Desperate Songstress* (literally translated as Crazy Songstress, 1990) and Zhou Xiaowen's *Desperation* (literally, Last Craziness, 1988) and *Obsession* (literally, The Price for Craziness, 1989), all emerged in the concluding years of the immediate post-Mao decade of the 1980s. They resemble contemporary urban-themed crime thrillers, dramatizing individuals tempted by the freedom of China's opening up to the outside world and by the materialist lure of the burgeoning market economy. Titles such as *Lust to Kill* (Canku de yuwang, 1988) and *Flames of Desire* (Yuwang the huoyan, 1988) added underpinning annotations to the meanings of being crazy then. Contrasting the *Crazy Stone* phenomenon of 2006, the cultural craziness showcased in the 1980s had a different era feel. Instead of sarcastic indulgence in cheers and jeers, instead of joking parodies bouncing in the wide expanse of either the cyber-connected world or what Desser calls "cinephilia" (the intertextual chain of filmic references, borrowings, and re-workings), and instead of a carnival revelry, the craziness showcased then was more like a morbid reaction induced by political traumas, a pubescent confusion of growing up in a cultural closure, and a hesitant rendezvous with craziness as a path to enrichment coupled with fear of the doom it may bring.

The word craziness in the late 1980s testified to the era's prevailing ideological effort to break the Maoist engineering of human norms. The contemporary cultural passion for *rehumanization* (renxing fugui) was described by literary theorist Li Zehou as an eruption that "all evolved around the liberation of the sensual, blood-and-flesh individuals from the tortures of a rationality that was turned into deity" (2008, 255). Appearing crazy was one of several artistic means used to break the overwhelming yoke of rationality. Commenting on this implication of the word in relation to Zhou Xiaowen's crazy-titled films, Jia Leilei, a scholar who participated in a panel discussion of Zhou's films, was reminded of *The Praise of Folly* (its literal translation from Chinese is *The Praise of Craziness*) by Desiderius Erasmus, the Dutch writer of the Renaissance era. As we know, this satirical book was a personification of ideas. Folly (Craziness), wearing the costume of a fool, spoke to a crowd and she, as Jia Leilei read it,

> makes the concept of craziness alive: she lives her life with no restrains, she indulges in carnivals with no worries, she jeers at the wickedness and hypocrisy of the clergies and nobilities with no fear ... Craziness [in this book]

becomes the synonym of joy and bliss. *The Praise of Craziness (Folly)* has virtually becomes a praise of humanity. (Yuan Ying et al. 1989, 87)

In contrast, Jia felt that the craziness showcased in Zhou's crazy-titled films back then was not as joyful and blissful. Rather, it was a perplexing, existential element that was beyond control of the film characters. Indeed, the craziness portrayed by Zhou was part and parcel of an absurdity shown in contemporary Chinese life. Zhou, as an admirer of modernist writer Franz Kafka, acknowledged the latter's impact on him in portraying crazi-ness, which needed to be absurd and traumatic (Chai Xiaofeng 1989, 83). In this sense, Zhou's craziness appeared a far cry from the classical sense of being crazy, as Plato and Socrates discussed it in the *Phaedrus* and the *Symposium*. Perceived not as illness, this craze, *Eros*, could be an expres-sion of the divine—it allowed human souls to grow wings—it showed humans the way to happiness and to appreciate beauty in life, and it welded humans to meaningful, loving relationships. Deep down, however, the crazy films of the 1980s hoped for the same, and it might well be based on this hope that their traumatic craziness was given cognitive value. Though not as joyful, craziness here was primarily meant for social and cultural critique. Li Yimin, another scholar at the same panel discussion, resorted to Michael Foucault to justify a society's need for craziness. He explained the existential potential of craziness harbored in the film under discus-sion—"every normal individual can become crazy in extraordinary condi-tions" (Yuan Ying et al. 1989, 87). Foucault's impact, it was interesting to note, had only just then started to be felt in China.[1]

Craziness of this kind offers us a unique perspective to understand modernism of the period. Modernism captures the zeitgeist of the 1980s, reflecting, as Zhang Xudong talks about it in an interview (Zhu Yu 2010), the collective anxiety of China's closure and lagging behind in the global arena and a general fascination with any antidotes for this closure. As dis-cussed in the introduction, the craziness of this era has an uncanny resem-blance to the basic connotation of the term in the West. In writing about the cultural contradictions of capitalism, Harvard scholar Daniel Bell believes that modernism contains a contradiction of rationality (the basic requirement of the capitalist system) versus an ever greater emphasis on such values as emotions, personal gratification, and the total fulfillment of the self. In China in the 1980s, *rehumanization* allowed the Chinese fash-ioning of modernism to showcase its confrontation with the contemporary political system. *Rehumanization* needs to dramatize freeing politicized human beings from rationality.

Rehumanization calls for an enriched understanding of human beings. Here emerges the 1980s' scholarly fascination with Herbert Marcuse, who, in the name of Marxism, rekindled the era's interest in Freud and in the psychological as well as philosophical complexity of being human. Since a 1979 article introducing Marcuse as a member of the Frankfurt School of Marxism in *Zhexue yicong* (Digest of Philosophy in Translation), scholarly articles and reviews on Marcuse mushroomed in the following years, particularly the late 1980s. In 1988, the translator of Marcuse's *Eros and Civilization* wrote in *Dushu* (Book Review) magazine that the book, which was to be published in the same year, is as important to Chinese readers for their renewed understanding of Marxism as the impact of Marx's *On Capital* is on traditional Marxism. In articles featuring Marcuse, such subtitles as "To liberate human beings is to liberate *eros*" (Xue Min 1988) well illustrate the era's need for Marcuse to help define liberation. The *rehumanization* demands of the time have led Chinese scholars to read their own situation into Marcuse's fascinating ideas, for example, about human nature, *Eros*, and liberation, as the Chinese scholars highlight them selectively[2]:

(1) To avoid defining humans in simplistic terms politically, it is reassuring to know that "precisely in his gratification, and especially in his sexual gratification, man was to be a higher being, committed to higher values; sexuality was to be dignified by love" (Marcuse 1966, 201); it is the unconscious human instincts and *Eros* that play more roles in defining human nature.

(2) The 1980s want to understand humans in complex conditions and welcome the idea that "liberated from the tyranny of repressive reason, the instincts tend toward free and lasting existential relations" (Marcuse 1966, 197).

(3) In a culture of liberation, sexuality's roles in life, culture and marketing become highly visible. It is encouraging to hear "sexuality tends to 'grow into' *Eros*—that is to say, toward self-sublimation in lasting and expanding relations" (Marcuse 1966, 222). "Eros, as life instinct, denotes a larger biological instinct rather than a larger scope of sexuality" (Marcuse 1966, 205).

(4) Still touching the wounds caused by antagonism of class-struggle ideology, it is fascinating for the 1980s to hear the ideas of "*Eros* as the builder of culture" (Marcuse, 213) and "the biological drive becomes a

cultural drive" (Marcuse 1966, 212). How nice that *Eros* can be conceived of "not as the repressive sublimation but as the free self-development" (Marcuse 1966, 125–6)!

(5) Having high hopes for arts and their roles to break the yokes, the Chinese are drawn to Marcuse's discussion of aesthetic imagination, which "in a free synthesis of its own", "constitutes beauty" (Marcuse 1966, 177). "The discipline of aesthetics," Marcuse also writes, "installs the *order of sensuousness* as against the *order of reason*. Introduced into the philosophy of culture, this notion aims at a liberation of the senses which, far from destroying civilization, would give it a firmer basis and would greatly enhance its potentialities" (Marcuse 1966, 181).

(6) Being iconoclastic, *rehumanization* is fascinated with Marcuse's use of alternative mythical figures to serve as archetypes for the future of mankind in a non-repressive culture. Replacing Prometheus (toil, productivity, and progress through repression) vs. Pandora (sexuality and pleasure taken as curse), Orpheus and Narcissus are now delivering different messages: "they recall the experience of a world that is not to be mastered and controlled but to be liberated—freedom that will release the powers of Eros." (Marcuse 1966, 164)

Although scholars of the 1980s see more illuminating dreams than feasibility in Marcuse, they appreciate the beauty and hopes they find in these dreams. One scholar describes himself as being awakened in a dark night, and he asks folks to join him to keep watch for the dawn, "when enlightened souls want to keep expecting and not falling asleep, there is hope after all" (Zhao Yuesheng 1988, 20).

To liberate humans, a more popular cultural influence in the 1980s was the Czech writer Milan Kundera, whose writing helped illustrate the ideological characteristics of our filmic showcasing of craziness. Records indicate that in the decade between 1987 and 1997, with two upheavals of popular following, most of Kundera's works were translated, some even in different versions, and the copies sold exceeded half a million (Li Fengliang 2001). In this popular reception loomed the start of de-sublimation and budding cynicism. The identical post-socialist history of China and Czechoslovakia that had both left behind an ideologue politics of totalitarian one-party rule based on monolithic structures of meanings made Kundera particularly appealing to the Chinese audience in the late 1980s.

Among his popular terms such as being, imagology, and *kitsch*, how *kitsch* was discussed in Kundera's best-known novel *The Unbearable*

Lightness of Being explained the existentialist tendency shown in the art of our selected films:

> *Kitsch* is the absolute denial of shit, in both the literal and the figurative senses of the word; kitsch excludes everything from its purview which is essentially unacceptable in human existence. (Kundera 1984, 248)

What involved to deviate from *kitsch*-controlled life was to turn from a protected innocence based on a monolithic value system to a daunting inclusion of "shitty" existential details that led to value relativity and cultural multiplicity. It was not going to be "a single political movement corners power" (Kundera 1984, 251); it was not going to be "all answers are given in advance and preclude any questions" (Kundera 1984, 254); and it was not going to continue to show films that were "saturated with incredible innocence and chastity" (Kundera 1984, 252–3). If we depicted this change like that from a protected childhood to the more independent, hormone-driven explorations in puberty, we understood more of the images and themes of youth and growth in our selected films, particularly in Zhou's *Obsession*.

Kundera's fictional style also appeared identical to the style of our selected films. As noticed by Terry Eagleton, the Kundera style was characterized by being plain, "without modernist outrage or obtrusiveness, utterly bereft of any intense aesthetic self-consciousness or portentous experimentalism" (Eagleton 1987, 27). The feature of this unadorned art was how it deviated from the "shitless" *kitsch*, which was noted for its "idealizing disavowal of the unacceptable" (Eagleton 1987, 31), and how it became more and more attentive to the existentialist details, which "refuses to fall back upon an unquestioning romantic idealism of the individual" (Eagleton 1987, 29). This anti-romantic approach might often appear "carnivalesque" since it rendered "romantic idealism to the point of absurdity" (Eagleton 1987, 29). Point to point, this depiction of the Kundera style also explained our crazy films, although the latter was more accessed in terms of the reigning cultural concerns for *rehumanization*. Paraphrasing *rehumanization*, however, revealed an underlying similarity: *rehumanization* meant a portrayal of the existentially situated individual instead of the ideologically romanticized individual. The effect of a plain style becoming carnivalesque in the 1980s, nonetheless, also contrasts the dominant carnivalesque feature of 2006 *Crazy Stone* phenomenon; the former derives more from the inclusion of existential details of everyday life and the latter relies more on aesthetic consciousness of experimentalism. The stylistic similarity between Kundera fiction and our films of the 1980s is not caused by mechanisms of a cinephilia, that is, media-induced influences. Rather, it is the similar ideological conditions that produced similar artistic responses.

By the same token, the culture of *rehumanization* also explains the accidental, stylistic similarity of our selected films in this chapter with traditional, American film noirs. "The appeal of film noir," as Winfried Fluck (2001, 404) observes, "reflects a value change in which traditional theories of the subject are replaced by a jubilant rhetoric of disintegration, because the older concepts are experienced as oppressive." The immediate post-Mao assessment with the social and cultural trauma and the era's fascination with the enigma of human nature produced similar noir films which usher in urbanism, feature crimes, confuse the line between ordinary folks and criminals, showcase enigmatic psychology of the crime, and deliver no explicit messages with philosophical depth. These films are much interested in producing a mood in which "the figure of the criminal became a metaphor for 'dark' dimensions of the self that remain incomprehensible" (Fluck 2001, 379). In these noir films, one witnesses similar artistic expressions owing to similar cultural needs, a parallelism that is meaningful enough to enhance each other's interpretation but shows no significant communication of influences between them.

Once the accidental noir feature of the films in this era is established, we need to consider its connection with the neo-noir features of the later, *Crazy Stone*-induced films. Here we have parallelism and real communication working together. First, there is a similar, logical development of noir turning to neo-noir, in the West as well as in China, because the "jubilant rhetoric of disintegration" (Fluck 2001, 404) plants seeds of playful cynicism. In the field of film production in China, there is a marked growth of playful cynicism between the late 1980s and 2006, when *Crazy Stone* was produced. This Chinese resemblance to the emergence of neo-noir in the west, primarily, still needs to be seen as an accidental parallelism. Second, in addition to social and cultural issues of post-socialism being represented and accessed in the name of postmodernism (one more example of parallelism), there are actually channels in which the Chinese neo-noir features connect with the cinematic culture of global neo-noir. There are cases testifying to the influences of Guy Ritchie, Quentin Tarantino, and the Cohen brothers. There is also the culturally trendy *egao* (mischievous parody) in Chinese film culture to actively build the network of references.

2   *DESPERATE SONGSTRESS:* COOL, ROCKING DARKNESS

We can't be sure if pop singer Mao Amin's selection to be the protagonist of *Desperate Songstress* (Fengkuang genü, 1988) is because of the popularity of her first album of 1985, *Hot Coffee* (Gunre de kafei). The lyrics of her music, nonetheless, might have predicted that she would end up in a noir film:

> Wandering on the neon-dazzling streets,
> The happy crowd there is not my world.
> Hot coffee can't warm my chilled heart,
> All because of you, you left me
> …
> I am helplessly alone on the street of the dark night.

Although it is Mao's other songs that are used in the film, the lyric here happens to describe the film's story. In a post-Mao metropolis teeming with newly liberated individuals yearning for romantic love, the songs of pop singer Wu Yani (played by Mao Amin) keep them spellbound. Wu herself, however, is aloof from the crowd, remaining a mysterious loner. While a journalist of an evening newspaper is determined to dig her story up, a police detective joins the investigation because of the singer's possible involvement with a recent murder case. The investigation causes the film to resemble the "traumatic" literature and film of the immediate post-Mao period close to a decade before: Wu is discovered to be an orphan left behind by a couple of political refugees to a mountain village. She is adopted by an old woman in the village and eventually becomes betrothed with the son of the woman. Upon being raped and killing her attacker in a struggle for self-defense, Wu flees the mountain village. When she tries to kill herself by lying on train rails, she is rescued by an artist who is exiled to the Mongolian grasslands. For years Wu lives on the grassland, falling in love with the land and the artist. She, nonetheless, has to keep her secret to herself and finally decides to run away from the artist to the city. She becomes successful as a singer but she fears to relate with her past.

Unfolding her history makes the film traumatic since the reason that keeps Wu from romantic love is caused by a political past. Investigating crime and determining guilt, however, attributes the film noir. Wu's dark dimension of self is not purely political now. She lacks courage to face her psychological trauma as a rape victim, and she is not resolute enough to cut herself off emotionally and legally from a past marriage arrangement to make room for her new romantic partner. She harbors her desire (there are steaming bathroom scenes in the film when she indulges into an illusion of seeing her partner) and hides behind her songs. Winfried Fluck (2001) believes that *film noir* differs from gangster films by drawing "ordinary" citizens into crime by accident, which focuses the audience's attention on the characters' accountability for the crime. This is what happens to Wu in *Desperate Songstress.* "To take this link between crime, guilt, and subjectivity as a point of departure (and comparison between different film noirs)," Fluck holds, "allows us to place film noir in the wider context of cultural history" (Fluck 2001, 383). For this film, the wider context is the transit from traumatic literature to a more existential re-configuring of human nature in the post-Mao China. Wu is indeed involved with the death of Changshun, her betrothed young man from the mountain, who has become rich in China's recent modernization and has managed to track Wu down in the city. While telling the frustrated, drunk Changshun that she can't return to her past, Wu notices that the fire of the gas stove in the room is blown out by the water spilled from a boiling kettle. Instead of turning off the gas, she turns it fully on and leaves the room—Changshun dies in the explosion when he lights his cigarette.

When Wu's involvement with Changshun's death is determined, the link between crime, guilt, and subjectivity really becomes a challenge to the audience, especially when it sees Wu choosing death to untangle the link, killing herself by lying on the train rails again. She did not die in the darkness of the political chaos of the past. She dies now for her songs. Here we touch upon one more attraction of film noir, which, "in its stylized theatricality, has found a way to transform 'self-dissolution' into a 'cool,' pleasurable experience" (Fluck 2001, 379). In *Desperate Songstress,* the concert scenes of Wu's songs are accompanied by the portrayal of her fans and scenes of street dancing and rock'n'roll gatherings. Just like rock culture has become a favorite subject of contemporary art films, such as Tian Zhuangzhuang's film *Rock Kids* (Yuaogun qingnian, 1988), it has also become profitable for so-called entertainment films (yule pian) of 1988, including *Desperate Songstress.* Zhou Xiaowen's *Desperation* (1987), which was marketed as an entertainment film, also uses strikingly similar scenes of street dancing and rock music to indicate the cultural pulse of the time. The cool feeling of songs and dances helps explain the craziness to which the film's Chinese title refers. To retain the cool experience of songs and dances, it is not only Wu who sacrifices her life for it, but also a fan in the film, who becomes Wu's alter ego, does the same. This taxi driver worships Wu's songs. He turns his apartment Wu's hall of fame. He follows Wu everywhere and thus becomes a witness to her guilt/crime (she should have a guilty conscience, but she is indeed legally difficult to incriminate). After learning Wu's story, he decides to die for her. He arranges to meet the artist and offers to take responsibility for the fatal explosion. Before he hands himself to the police, however, he leads them on a chase. Police cars, sirens blaring, chasing a young man on a motorcycle is indeed an important element for film entertainment. What is subtle in the choreography of this chase scene is that the pursued had his chance to "street dance" on a motorcycle before surrendering. In the meantime, Wu is surprised to be joined by the artist. She has her obvious first sex with him and then walks away to her death—"as she emerged with her songs" the film's voice-over explains, "she dies in her songs" (Fig. 2.1).

Fig. 2.1 *Desperate Songstress.* "As she emerged with her songs, she dies in her songs"

3   *DESPERATION*: SELF-CHASING AND EXISTENTIAL MODERNISM

The sense of darkness in *Desperation* (Zuihou de fengkang, 1987) is sustained by the similarities of the police detective and the fugitive, which reflects the film's effort to blur the line between the guilty and innocent. *Desperation* is an action thriller of a detective on the trail of a fugitive who is at large after killing police and who makes his capture even more difficult by possessing explosives. The film attracts the audience by the wit, calculation, and adroitness of the action of either the hunter or the hunted in the pursuit. It has plenty of essential elements of the genre such as car chases, the use of motorcycles and helicopters, as well as showcasing surveillance equipment. More important, however, it reveals the uncanny similarities of the hunter and the hunted in the process: they both have military backgrounds; they are both tough guys who tend to become confrontational in their social interactions; yet they are also both tender in their respect for their fathers (they both lost mothers when they were young) and in their love for their girlfriends.[3] Toward the end of the film, neither wins; they die together in an explosion. Although this arrangement of characterization is open to social interpretations, that is, how their respective stories show their confrontation with the system and their dislocation in social change, their similarity remains hauntingly allegorical of the mysterious human nature that makes them each other's alter ego. This design, according to Zhou Xiaowen, is to create a psychological implication of human nature: although the story appears to be a police officer hunting down a fugitive, it is actually also about a person chasing his own shadow—"in sub-consciousness," Zhou explains, "everyone relentlessly chases the self without even knowing it" (Fang Zhou 2007, 43) (Fig. 2.2).

This pursuit offers us existential glimpses of *rehumanization*, which wants to showcase humans alive, in response to complex desires to live. The characters in the film, in their mutual reference, produce a generally shared feeling of liberation that is accompanied by yearning and excitement, which, as the title of the film suggests, may also be called a touch of craziness. Some reviewers felt that the story of the first half of the film is not well organized, that it appears to be wandering. Yet, it is exactly this wandering in preparation for the police hunt, as if it is a European *flâneur* walking and discovering the cultural map of a city, that offers the audience the context of the chase.[4] A magazine kiosk attracts attention by showcasing not only the much-publicized fetishizing of enigmatic female beauty

Fig. 2.2 *Desperation*. Police and fugitive; a person chasing his own shadow

(a crucial component of *rehumanization*), but also how tidbits of the out-side world emerge to cater to the eager curiosity of the masses. Here lies an accidental similarity with a "distinguishing feature of the centrifugal noir" in showing "the importance of communication networks and the mass media as substitutes for recognizable visible landmarks" (Frey 2006, 67).[5] The magazine kiosk represents the budding importance of mass media in China's contemporary cultural scene. Background scenes during police searches offer the audience glimpses of an artist's superb street dancing performance, girls in fancy swimming suits on beach, and cus-tomers getting their hair styled in a salon, as well as petty criminals shoot-ing erotic videos. The fugitives on the run also allow the audience to see busy shopping plazas, tasteful restaurants, high-end real estate, and fash-ionable young women. In line with the contemporary Chinese cinematic rejection of docile, feminized males and its fascination with new masculine icons in rebels and tough guys, both the detective and the fugitive are portrayed as "attractive" men—there are two corresponding sequences in which they kiss their girlfriends passionately.

With all these cultural impulses used as backdrops, *Desperation* joins contemporary Fifth Generation breakthrough films in featuring unconventional characters. The similarity between the police and the fugitive suggests a thin, blurred line that separates an ordinary person and a criminal. Another film issued in the same year by Xi'an Film Studio, *Red Sorghum*, also testifies to this same fascination: in a love story of unconventional characters, human nature and nationalism connect such diversified characters as farmhands, communists, and bandits in their heroic action against Japanese invasion. It is interesting to note that *Desperation* and *Red Sorghum* were promoted by Xi'an Studio as their two most innovative films of the year.

Whereas the two films are similar in unconventional characterization, they illustrate two different cultural orientations. By winning the Golden Bear in Berlin in 1988, *Red Sorghum* has become internationally better known, and it remains a representative film of the Fifth Generation cultural critique, characterized by cultural retrospection and roots searching. This type of cultural critique harbors the hope for cultural resurrection; it encloses the artists and intellectuals in nationalism, and burdens them with the responsibility of helping to create the new cultural totality. This cultural nationalism, as described by a Chinese scholar Ge Hua, is like "a desperate maze and imprisonment" for the Chinese artists and intellectuals of the 1980s (1994, 37). What distinguishes director Zhou Xiaowen from this orientation, according to Ge, is his "sense of modernity" (Ge Hua 1994, 37). This sense of modernity is not the same modernity that the Party was promoting (e.g., the campaign of the four kinds of modernization of China), nor it is that implied by the cultural roots searching when it features the theme of modernity versus primitivism. This sort of "modernity," Ge writes, "is not a completely new historical encounter … nor is it a genesis in contemporary Chinese historical narrative. Rather, it is more like an existential status for the contemporary Chinese" (Ge Hua 1994, 37). It is this modernity that renders Zhou Xiaowen "a contemporary urbanite and a pure film artist" (Ge Hua 1994, 37). Obviously, one can understand this sense of modernity as existential modernism.

If *Red Sorghum* has become a representative work of cultural nationalism, *Desperation* is that for existential modernism, which is also showcased in Huang Jianxin's contemporary, urban subject films and picked up by many Sixth Generation-directed films known for their gritty, urban realism. These films' resemblance to film noir pops up again, more focused on the impact of André Bazin and existentialism in the noir discourse. Concerning these impacts, James Naremore identifies how French post-war critics "project Bazin's ideas onto films noirs" to highlight "the triumph of interiorization and ambiguity":

> the themes of isolation, uncertainty and ambiguity must have exerted a strong appeal to anyone who was wary of collective politics and inclined to treat social issues in terms of personal ethics. (Naremore 95–96, 23)

Naremore's discussion offers insight for understanding the emergence of existential modernism in China and how a similar transition from political oppression to personal ethics help constitute similar noir features in Chinese films. Even the roles played by Bazin in the making of film noir discourse in the West and in the budding existential modernism in Chinese cinema appear similar since *rehumanization* in China was also seeking the triumph of interiorization and ambiguity. Whereas the scholarly effort to introduce Bazin in China in 1962 met with little response, post-Mao *rehumanization* culture embraced Bazin.[6] Bazin was invoked for the "modernization" of Chinese film language; he was projected first in the promotion of the Fourth Generation directors' "documentary aesthetics" and later in other versions of "personalism" and realism that discover an under-represented subject matter, respect ethical complexity, and work toward de-sublimation.

What further distinguished *Desperation* as Xi'an Studio's innovation of the year was its attention to the market, Zhou's publicized effort "to tear down the wall between entertainment film and art film" with the production of this film, and contemporary film criticism's endorsement of the idea. This breakthrough is actually within the range of exerting existential modernism. Even the comparison with the general cultural orientation shown in Western noir discourse still remains meaningful. Whereas Western film noirs contribute to "the destruction of bourgeois art and the desublimation of everyday life" (Naremore 2008, 18), de-sublimation in China in the 1980s calls for broadening the scope of art and for becoming more attentive to mass culture. It problematized the deep-rooted cultural concept of "*wen yi zai dao*" (artworks need to be vehicles for grand truth) and looked into how the concept had strictly allowed only a narrow range of subjects to be considered art. The broadened concept of art and the due respect for the market has not only helped showcase the modernist craziness in the 1980s but also paved the way for the *Crazy Stone* phenomenon to occur later.

4   *OBSESSION*: ACTIVATING CULTURAL PSYCHOANALYSIS

The production of *Obsession* (Fengkuang de daijia, 1989) was based on the success of *Desperation*, which in 1988 won both the Golden Rooster Award and the Government Award (by the Central Commission of Radio, TV, and Films). Although the Golden Rooster Award is mostly based on a popularity poll, 1988 was the first time it had ever been given to a "commercial film" (Rong Weiqian 1994, 46). Timing appeared right for what Zhou Xiaowen was doing in name of box office and entertainment. While deciding about his next assignment, his studio boss Wu Tianming pointed out half-jokingly that Zhou had become an icon for commercial film and that he should not pick anything like *Life on a String* (Zhou's own proposal) but something resembling *Desperation*.[7] The result was *Obsession*.

Although the studio insisted that *Obsession* still needed to be a detective film involving police action, Zhou was more attracted by the characterization of his previous film, that is, the similarity of the detective and the fugitive and the subtle role played by pursuit to connect the characters. Zhou mentioned that he was impressed by a French friend's interpretation of *Desperation* as a film of love (*Eros*)—the policeman's hunt of the criminal is a man's search for love, search for another man that is his alter ego, with the desperation that leads the two to die together in an explosion (Chai Xiaofeng 1989, 77). In *Obsession*, a film about the police investigation of a rape case (a young man offers an underage girl a ride, rapes her, and abandons her), Zhou develops more evolved characters connected by the crime. On the one side, there are two sisters: Lanlan, the teenage victim of rape, and Qingqing, her sister and guardian, a gynecologist who is possessed by an obsession (what gives the film its title) to hunt down and to retaliate against the rapist. She eventually kicks the rapist down the stairs of a high tower when he is captured by police and, in doing so, turns herself into a killer. On the other side, there are two brothers: Sun Dacheng, the rapist, and his elder brother and guardian, Sun Dasheng, a mechanic. The crime is committed against the backdrop of 1980s *rehumanization* culture, in which sexuality has turned from a taboo that had little room in art or public discourse to not only a fascinating topic for discussion but also a commodity used to promote sales of related publications. The crime anchors the characterization and gender portrayal of the film.

The film depicts the two brothers and two sisters as limited in their understanding of sexuality and gender specificity; they, after all, have grown up in a culture in which these issues are not talked about. The *mise en scène*

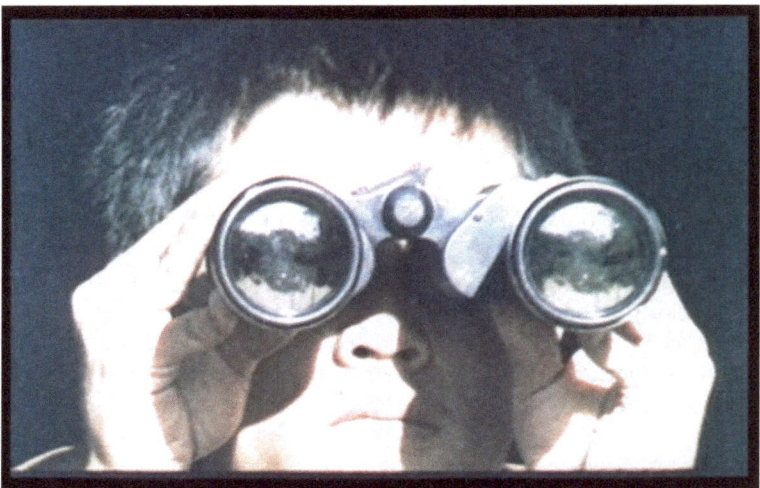

Fig. 2.3 *Obsession.* Yearning and fear; male anxiety

of the film depicts the two brothers' life as both yearning and fearing women (Fig. 2.3). They live in a room in a high-rise building. The younger brother enjoys reading erotic books and uses his telescope to spy on neighbors. The decor of their room is all masculine: muscle-building fitness equipment is the central piece of furniture, and the posters on the wall are those of motorcycles and action star Sylvester Stallone. What the elder brother imposes on the younger brother is the masculine code of martial arts, typified by the Chinese classical novel, *On the Water Margin*, in which all the rebel brothers swear to avoid women and use martial arts as well as alcohol as the alternative for their fulfillment. Here the need for women is covered up by the lack of understanding of and thus fear of women. In the film, the younger brother is equally confused and baffled by his attraction to women; he has the urge enough to commit the crime of rape, but later in the film, when a mature woman at a magazine kiosk flirts with him, he is so baffled that he flees. He confesses to his elder brother that he wishes there were no gender differences among human beings.

The two sisters are equally underprepared for sexuality in their lives. Whereas the younger sister is forced to confront sexuality when she is neither physically nor psychologically mature enough for it, her elder sister is unmarried and filled with anxiety of what to do with her persistent suitor in particular and men in general. Zhou instructs the actress playing this role to use her body language to indicate that she has had no sexual experience with men, yet she has a physical yearning for man (indicated by two photos of Stallone hidden in her closet), and her job in the hospital has exposed her so often to the sexist culture of China that she has learned to hate men for their ability to take advantage of women. The film starts and ends with the two sisters in a public spa. Their soft, amorous touches of each other choreographed with shots filtered by water drops and warm steam has impressed filmgoers so much that they keep referring to the footages as "murky beauty of femininity" (in reference to contemporary popularity of murky poetry, *monglong shi*). This beginning and ending, in addition to helping contrast gender differences in *mise en scène*, adds a sad touch to the film. As one reviewer observes, if the beginning shows a vision of "utopia of gender harmony," the ending is a "sigh for its disappearance" (Yuan Ying et al. 1989, 90). The two sisters are both damaged in the story: the younger sister is raped and becomes disillusioned (she blows a big bulb of gum toward the camera at the news of her sister's retaliation of the rapist) and the elder sister incriminates herself through the revenge (Fig. 2.4).

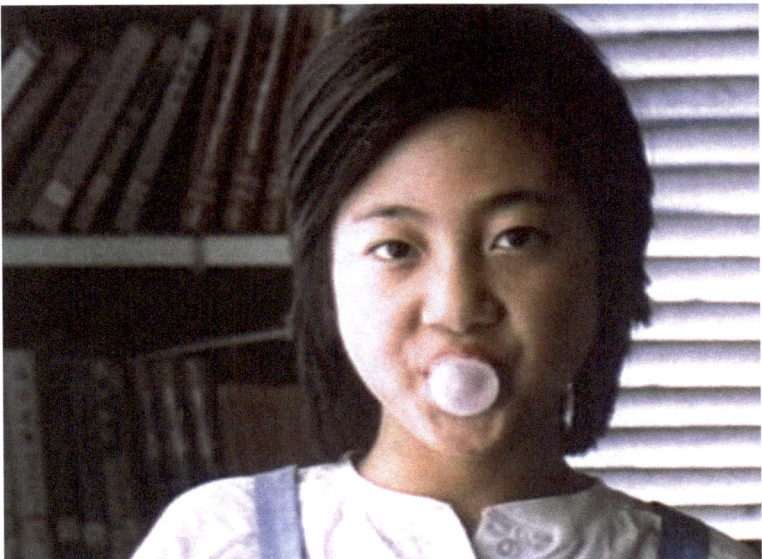

Fig. 2.4 *Obsession*. The rape victim becomes disillusioned

The film captured critical attention the moment it came out. Seeing it as a new type of crime thriller that is "minutely done in naturalism," "both rational and sensual," and changes from showing "gender confrontation" to "gender confusion" (Yuan Ying et al. 1989, 85), scholars were fascinated by the film and offered it a status that had never been given to a commercial film—China's leading journal *Contemporary Cinema* organized and published a panel discussion of this film by experts in the field. Reflecting China's opening up and leading scholars' eagerness for new ideas, the academic access of *Obsession* reached for topics that were not often covered in common discourse and appeared rather unique and *avant-garde*. Some of these ideas, for example, concern gender, feminism, and the rising role of the market in manipulating trendy discourse.

Zhang Wei, a male scholar, argues that the film touches upon a feminist idea of androgyny represented not only by the perplexed confession of the rapist but also by the retaliation of Qingqing, who assumes a male role that is usually filled by either a policeman or a father. The whole film indicates androgyny since it has allowed women "to utter their dissatisfaction with men as a whole," and objectively portrays certain female perspectives but also naturally assumes a male understanding of the world (Yuan Ying et al. 1989, 93). Li Yimin, another male scholar, asserts that seen in perspectives of feminism and psychoanalysis, Qingqing's revenge "is a twofold process of female victim steps into the shoes of a male victimizer, or a castrated female in search of a potent male" (Yuan Ying et al. 1989, 86). Zhong Li, also a male scholar, finds fault with this male-directed "female attempt to dismantle the male-centered culture," believing that "it has achieved very little except causing some temporary fear in males of castration" and in the end "females still undress and get into the spa and the male audience still gaze with desire in comfort" (Yuan Ying et al. 1989, 88). A female scholar, Dai Jinhua, endorses her colleagues' gender-specific observations and emphasizes the psychoanalytic approaches of the film, believing that an understanding of Qingqing's abnormal psyche may benefit from Freudian dream analysis; Qingqing's story, in manifest content, "configures super ego, the punitive forces of society, justice and ethics" but, in latent content, she is shown as driven by a confused psyche that is triggered by the event of her sister's rape to get into "a series of obsessive actions that reveal her desire/fear as well as need/hatred for man" (Yuan Ying et al. 1989, 91). She also notices that Qingqing is from a family with neither mother nor father figures, which further contributes to her abnormal psyche since even the Oedipus complex is not playing enough role in her coming of age.

Dai's opinions about this film offer us a reference point of not only the elite feature of the scholarly perspectives of the film we have just sampled but also how it contrasts to a common discourse that lacks attention to gender specificity, and how it may strongly impact common discourse in the *rehumanization* era. Only a year before, Dai promoted a feminist reading of Huang Shuqin's *Woman, Human, Demon* (Ren gui qing, 1988). The film, at its premier in China, was accessed by critics primarily on non-gender-specific features such as the representation of demons and the related *rehumanization* theme that human nature may contain evil touches (ren xing e). However, when shown at the Créteil International Women's Film Festival in France, it was acclaimed as thoroughly feminist. Dai bridged this gap of difference in reception. With the introduction of Western feminism in literary and film criticism in the late 1980s as a backdrop,[8] Dai's convincing feminist reading of *Woman, Human, Demon* fascinated the director Huang Shuqin herself, who had known nothing about feminism while directing the film but fell in love with talking about it since. In retrospect, Huang reflects,

> There are two reasons why our critics don't talk about feminist films. First, Chinese society discourages feminist consciousness; nobody bothers with it. Second, critics believe that the "feminist consciousness" limits and even demeans our understanding of a particular film. 'Till now, people have been advising me not to talk about my films as feminist so that they might be understood on a higher level. (Kuoshu 2002, 131)

In promoting feminist reading of *Woman, Demon, Human*, Dai was still a rather lonesome voice. In the critical access of *Obsession*, in contrast, her voice had merged with a rich symphony of similar ideas.

Dai's observation of the lack of father figure in the film was raised as a psychoanalytic element. It was soon elaborated by Li Yimin, who was also at the panel discussion, in a 1989 article almost solely referencing Marcuse's *Eros and Civilization*. The article used the absence of father figures in a group of contemporary Chinese films, including *Obsession*, to illustrate the cultural implications of modernity in China then: China started a modernity process since the 1970s with the emergence of urban culture, mass media, and consumerism, indicating a transit from political mythology represented by father figures to an industrialized mythology shaped by mass media. In this context, the Oedipus complex is collective and cultural. It starts with political anxiety; "peoples' critique of totalitarian politics and yearning for more sage rulers are all based on the mythology represented by father figures" (Li Yiming 1989, 10). Soon, as mass media and consumerism take over, the traditional father figures become less relevant, as Li quotes Marcuse to prove,

> The experts of the mass media transmit the required values; they offer the perfect training in efficiency, toughness, personality, dream, and romance. With this education, the family can no longer compete. In the struggle between the generations, the sides seem to be shifted: the son knows better; he represents the mature reality principle against its obsolescent paternal forms ... [Father's] authority as transmitter of wealth, skills, experiences is greatly reduced; he has less to offer, and therefore less to prohibit. (Marcuse 1966, 97)

In the selected group of films, Li sees young protagonists given family space without parents to unfold their stories and argues that these lonesome characters dramatize their sociological as well as psychological adjustments to the transit just mentioned.

Li's heavy reference to Marcuse brings us back to our discussion of *rehumanization* culture at the beginning of this chapter. It has offered an important perspective in understanding the craziness of this era. It has also rehearsed a connection that is going to be an outstanding feature of the *Crazy Stone* phenomenon about two decades later, that is, the connection between the elite culture and the popular culture—the seemingly *avant-garde* theories heeding the low brow and the profane.

NOTES

1. Foucault's introduction in China started in 1984, when an article featuring his death was published in the scholarly journal *Social Sciences Abroad*. Since then, about a dozen articles were published in China in the 1980s discussing Foucault's ideas. Translation of Foucault's works started in the late 1980s: two versions of *The History of Sexuality* came out in 1988 and 1989, and *The Madness and Civilization* came out in 1990.

2. The following points are taken from contemporary Chinese articles on Marcuse. See Zhao Yuesheng (1988), Xue Min (1988), and Yang Xiaobin (1989).

3. The female characters in this story appear to be a far cry from the *femme fatale* in traditional Western noir films. They function more to indicate the hidden capability for love and tenderness in their male counterparts.

4. See Anke Gleber, *The Art of Taking a Walk: Flânerie, Literature, and Film in Weimar Culture* (Princeton University Press, 1999). The art of walking involves forms of spatial practice adopted by European intelligentsia as subversive tactics to combat alienation in urban life in the West.

5. This feature, indicating the importance of mass media, is first discussed in Dimendberg's book *Film Noir and the Spaces of Modernity* (Harvard University Press, 2004).

6. For a brief survey of Bazin's introduction in China, see Zheng Dongtian (2008).

7. Noted for its philosophical lyricism, *Life on a String* (Ming ruo qinxian) is a novel by Shi Tiesheng. As correctly predicted by Wu Tianming (head of Xi'an Studio) in his conversation with Zhou Xiaowen, it was adapted into a film by Chen Kaige in 1991.

8. According to Zhang Yanbin's *Nüquan zhuyi wenlun* (Feminist literary theory, Shandong jiaoyu chubanshe, 1998), 1988 saw a rise in the numbers of articles introducing Western literary feminism—about twenty, twice that of the previous two years. In 1988, *Dangdai dianying* (Contemporary Cinema), a scholarly journal, featured a special section on feminism in film studies in its sixth issue.

REFERENCES

CHINESE LANGUAGE SOURCES

Chai Xiaofeng. 1989. Huashuo *fengkuang de daijia*: yu zhou xiaowen duihua lu (Concerning *Obsession*: A Dialogue with Zhou Xiaowen). *Dangdai dianying* (Contemporary Cinema) 2: 75–84.

Fang Zhou. 2007. Zhou Xiaowen koushu: 'Fengkuang'de dianying shidai (Zhou Xiaowen Testimony: Crazy Era of Film Production). *Dazhong dianying* (Popular Cinema) 21: 42–45.

Ge Hua. 1994. Mimang zhi lu: chongdu Zhou Xiaowen (A Journey of Confusion: Reread Zhou Xiaowen). *Dangdai dianying* (Contemporary Cinema) 5: 37–44.

Li Fengliang. 2001. Jieshou Kundela: jiedu yu wudu (Kundera Reception: Reading and Misreading). *Guowai wenxue* (Foreign Literature) 81–82: 58–69.

Li Yiming. 1989. Shifu xingwei zhi hou: dangdai dianying zhong de jiating queshi yu buchang (With Fathers Being Slain: The Loss of Families and Its Compensation in Contemporary Chinese Films). *Dianying yishu* (Film Arts) 6: 9–18.

Li Zehou. 2008. *Zhongguo xiandai sixiangshi lun* (On Contemporary Chinese Intellectual History). Beijing: Sanlian shudian.

Rong Weiqian. 1994. Zhou Xiaowen: bei dianying kesi de daoyan (Zhou Xiaowen: A Dead-Serious Director About Films). *Dianying yishu* (Film Arts) 5: 45–49.

Xue Min. 1988. Maerkusai de 'aiyu jiefang lun' shuping (On Marcuse's Liberation of *Eros*). *Fudan xuebao, shehui kexue ban* (Fudan University Journal—Social Science Edition) 5: 107–111.

Yang Xiaobin. 1989. Yishu de aiyu xiangdu: Maerkusai yu shenmei geming (Love Orientation of Arts: Marcuse and a Revolution in Aesthetics). *Shanghai shehui kexueyuan xueshu jikan* (Scholarship Quarterly of Shanghai Academy of Social Sciences) 21 (2): 175–184.

Yuan Ying, et al. 1989. Fengkuang de daijia bitan (Panel Discussion of *Obsession*). *Dangdai dianying* (Contemporary Cinema) 2: 85–94.

Zhao Yuesheng. 1988. Zou xiang wuyayi wenming: du *aiyu yu wenming* (Towards a Non-Repressive Civilization: Reading *Eros and Civilization*). *Dushu* (Book Review) 8: 12–21.

Zheng Dongtian. 2008. Yiqun zhongguo nianqing dianyingren yu yige waiguo zhizhe de shengjiao (The Spiritual Exchange Between a Group of Chinese Young People and a Foreign Wise Man). *Dangdai dianying* (Contemporary Cinema) 4: 4–6.

Zhu Yu. 2010. Cong 'xiandai zhuyi' dao 'wenhua zhengzhi': Zhang Xudong jiaoshou fangtan lu (From "Modernism" to "Cultural Politics": An Interview of Professor Xudong Zhang). *Xiandai zhongwen xuekan* (Journal of Modern Chinese) 3–6: 4–27.

ENGLISH LANGUAGE SOURCES

Eagleton, Terry. 1987. Estrangement and Irony. *Salmagundi*, Special Issue, Milan Kundera: Fictive Lightness. Fictive Weight, 73 (Winter): 25–32.

Fluck, Winfried. 2001. Crime, Guilt, and Subjectivity in *Film Noir*. *Amerikastudien/ American Studies* 46 (3): 379–408.

Frey, Mattias. 2006. No(ir) Place to Go: Spatial Anxiety and Sartorial Intertextuality in 'Die Unberührbare'. *Cinema Journal* 45 (4): 64–80.

Kundera, Milan. 1984. *The Unbearable Lightness of Being* (Translated from the Czech by Michael Henry Heim). New York: Harper Perennial.

Kuoshu, Harry. 2002. *Celluloid China: Cinematic Encounters with Culture and Society.* Carbondale/Edwardsville: Southern Illinois University Press.

Marcuse, Herbert. 1966. *Eros and Civilization: A Philosophical Inquiry into Freud.* Boston: Beacon Press.

Naremore, James. 2008. *More Than Night: Film Noir in Its Contexts.* Updated and Expanded Edition. Berkeley: University of California Press.

CHAPTER 3

Discourses: *Crazy Stone* Dropped in a Postmodern Pond

Abstract The 2006 cultural carnival induced by the film *Crazy Stone* has not only prompted many films of similar styles but also showcased a network of ideas that makes the appearance of this film a particularly interesting juncture in the recent history of Chinese cinema as well as ideas. The metaphor is that the film is really like a piece of stone and its ability to cause craziness is attributed to its "postmodern" peculiarities; the contemporary cultural discourses are like a pond, fertile and ready to spread the ripples caused by the casting in of this peculiar stone. In light of this metaphor, this chapter draws a road map of discourses in topics of postmodernism, grassroots, carnival, and *egao* (mischievous parody).

Keywords Postmodernism • Post-emotionalism • Petty bourgeoisie • Grassroots • Carnival • *Egao* • Youth culture

Considering James Naremore's insightful assertion that film noir "belongs to the history of ideas as much as to the history of cinema" (1995–96, 14), one is intrigued to discover that the 2006 cultural carnival induced by the film *Crazy Stone* has not only prompted many films of similar styles but also showcased a network of ideas that makes the appearance of this film a particularly interesting juncture in the recent history of Chinese cinema as well as ideas. The metaphor is that the film is really like a piece of stone

© The Author(s), under exclusive license to Springer Nature Switzerland AG 2021
H. H. Kuoshu, *Craziness and Carnival in Neo-Noir Chinese Cinema*, Chinese Literature and Culture in the World, https://doi.org/10.1007/978-3-030-73081-9_3

and its ability to cause craziness is attributed to its "postmodern" pecu-liarities; the contemporary cultural discourses are like a pond, fertile and ready to spread the ripples caused by the casting in of this peculiar stone. To better understand this episode of cinema and ideas, a road map of top-ics of related discourses is called for.

1   POSTMODERNISM

Postmodernism arrived in China in the early 1980s through several intro-ductory articles.[1] In 1985, Frederic Jameson visited Beijing University to deliver and publish a series of lectures on postmodernism, which greatly promoted its visibility in China. However, since modernism represented such core intellectual concerns of the 1980s as *rehumanization*, cultural retrospection, and roots searching, interest in postmodernism remained a scholarly curiosity. With the Tian'anmen Square massacre as a watershed, the 1990s had a different feel. "Because of a catastrophic impact of a political turbulence," China's leading postmodernist advocate Wang Yuechuan writes, "Chinese intelligentsia moved into a period of depres-sion. Many of them, in having a deep retrospection of the radical theories and utopian complexes of the 1980s, acquired new resources and points of entry to their issues from postmodernism" (Wang Yuechuan 2001, 121). The 1990s witnessed not only a large-scale, systematic translation of postmodernist works from the West but also an increase in Chinese schol-ars' own studies on the topic, applying postmodernism to the analysis of Chinese issues.[2] Although there were doubts that the philosophy was applicable to China, the 1990s on the whole saw a high tide of interest in postmodernism. From the late 1990s to the early years of the twenty-first century, Chinese interest in postmodernism faded significantly, leading many to declare postmodernism passé in China. In the meantime, serious scholars became attentive to Western adjustments in understanding post-modernism, that is, from deconstructive to constructive postmodernism. They saw in this adjustment a chance to rejuvenate the use of postmodern-ism in China.

Many of these scholars welcomed *Crazy Stone* and the carnival of 2006 as vindication for the existence of postmodernism in China. In a panel discussion of *Crazy Stone* upon its release, Zhang Yiwu defined the film's postmodern features that would be reiterated in many later reviews: "ceaseless ironic dialogues, a narrative that remains superficial, and the copying of various films that appears either a salute to or jeering at them"

(Zheng Dongtian et al. 2006). Zhang believed that although *Crazy Stone* was only a partial testimony to postmodernity in China, it was already strong enough to remove the doubt raised by many in the past decade on whether postmodernism could develop in China. "To this issue that still needed discussion years back," Zhang wrote, "the history's testimony now is so forceful" (Zheng Dongtian et al. 2006).

Post-Mao China witnessed great value confusion in its transformation from a totalitarian ideological monopoly to a modern mixture of competing philosophies. To the Chinese critics, postmodernism best explains this situation and people's adjustment to it. One review of *Crazy Stone* reads,

> "God is dead" declares the cancellation of all values and beliefs, which, in a rational world, sustain subjectivity but in postmodern world they become fabrications and are no longer the shelter for subjectivity. Postmodernist art works testify to this kind of awkwardness of human existence. In the story of *Crazy Stone*, postmodernism cancels fixed values related with subjectivity. (Jiang Tianping and Xia Yiyun 2007, 149)

In postmodernism, the subjectivity becomes homeless. In exile, it is often plunged into a playful narrative, which in comparison with traditional, serious, drama-category narratives may appear shallow and not equally soul-touching. The issue here is actually de-sublimation, which often helps distinguish cultural rebels. Concerning this issue, another critic of *Crazy Stone* writes,

> The sublimation that the mainstream culture cares is avoided. Even the distinction between virtue and evil is vague … (the film) cancels heroes in the traditional sense … purposefully avoided value judgment. It allows the audience to see a profane living in multiplicity where the sociological distinction between 'heroes' and 'thieves' is replaced by a leveled existential status. (Liu Xueming 2007, 33)

To be postmodern is to break the monopoly of any controlling myth, be it the older Maoist socialist ideology of equality or the new, post-Mao myth that tolerating the creation of individual wealth eventually benefits public welfare. Critic Li Shengtao considers the monopoly of this kind of ideology the same as what Herbert Marcuse once detected in capitalist modernism: how it created one-dimensional humans who are locked in a one-dimensional society which produced the false need for people to recognize themselves in commodities. In this sense, to call *Crazy Stone* postmodern at least has two implications in association to Herbert Marcuse's earlier ideas of breaking the one-dimensional society. First, *Crazy Stone* is the kind of *avant-garde* art that Marcuse believes can help shatter the myths produced by the one-dimensional society. Second, *Crazy Stone*—and the Chinese discourse about it—is produced out of an alliance between radical intellectuals and socially marginalized groups, in whom Marcuse put his faith for moving away from the one-dimensional society.

The sense of exile and homelessness among contemporary Chinese is not expressed in tragedy but in black humor, which to Chinese critic Chen Xi has to do with the distinction between modernism and postmodernism. Chen Xi elaborates the distinction based on his reading of Daniel Bell's *The Cultural Contradictions of Capitalism* through translation:

> Traditional modernism, no matter how daring, played out its impulses in the imagination, within the constraints of art. Whether demonic or murderous, the fantasies were expressed through the ordering principle of aesthetic form. Art, therefore, even though subversive of society, still ranged itself on the side of order and, implicitly, of a rationality of form, if not of content. Post-modernism overflows the vessels of art. It tears down the boundaries and insists that *acting out*, rather than making distinctions, is the way to gain knowledge. (Quoted in Chen Xi 2011, 3; Bell 1976, 51–52)

From this passage, Chen Xi develops the contrast of comedy versus tragedy, multiplicity versus singularity, the accidental versus certainty, playfulness versus seriousness, and postmodern versus modern. One need not challenge if the model is too neat to be valid. What is of interest is how this chart helps illustrate the Chinese effort in justifying the need for postmodernism.

2   GRASSROOTS

If postmodernism is a political statement cloaked in a scholarly outfit, the next most prominent topic in the discourse, *Crazy Stone*'s connection with the grassroots, is asserting a widening appeal of this political statement. In the same 2006 panel discussion on *Crazy Stone* mentioned earlier, Zhang Yiwu pointed out the need to redefine the concept of the grassroots, and he believes that the bulk of the grassroots of contemporary China consists of what he terms *hou xiaozi* (post petty bourgeois). The concept plugs in Chinese scholars' interests in postmodernism as well as their attention to

Western efforts in updating traditional Marxist concepts in postmodern context, as French scholar Pierre Bourdieu does in defining the "new petty bourgeoisie."[3] In Zhang's explanation of this concept, one can see his effort to connect the outdated, ideological concept of the masses (*qunzhong*) with recent subcultural trends; the masses nowadays are primarily cyber creatures who populate China's mediascape.

Zhang's effort has a fairly important ideological implication. The concept of the masses has been the cornerstone of the Maoist social revolution theory. The existence of the masses testifies to the social antagonism between the oppressor and the oppressed and thus justifies the need for the Party on behalf of the masses and the Party's revolutionary agendas. Since the founding of the PRC, when the Party started to rule the nation, the actual social structure of the Party as the rulers (the potential oppressor) and people as the ruled (the potential oppressed) rendered the meaning of the masses vague. One wonders how long China can maintain the myth of being a Utopian state with a handful of class enemies controlled by the Party, which is supported by the overwhelming majority of the masses. Now this myth is being undermined by thinking of the masses primarily from the perspectives of Chinese youth. In post-Mao China, cultural deviation has been detected in diversified trends of youth subculture. The successive emergence of Generation *Ku*, *xiaozi* (petty bourgeoisie), and Generation Q has been compared to the fleeting, successive appearance of American youth subculture since 1960s such as Beatle fans, Hippies, Yuppies, and Preppies (Gong Changyu 2002, 72). The similarity here is actually attributed to postmodernism: since 1960, America witnessed the arrival of postmodernism along with all the pains caused by "capitalist cultural rupture"; since the 1990s, China also experienced postmodernism in "an all-around transformation" from closed, rural society with planned economy to open, urban society with globalized market economy (Gong Changyu 2002, 72). Young people are more sensitive to change and most attracted to postmodernism; "postmodernist challenges to center, order, and sole authority, as well as postmodernist ideas of multiplicity, equality, tolerance, and anti-tradition," all helped formulate Chinese youth subculture (Hong Xiaonan and Li Yan 2010, 36).

Before looking into the implication of Zhang's concept of post petty bourgeoisie, it should worth our while to survey briefly the major trends in Chinese youth subculture. Generation *Ku* is China's millennial generation (Hooper 1991; Marr and Rosen 1998; Moore 2005), which acquired its name by referring to American slang "cool" (detached, knowing, and in control) and Chinese character *"ku"* (cruel, keeping real feelings concealed, individualistic, and competent). Since the name of a trend may often derive from slang, it is important to understand that,

> Slang lexemes function differently from most standard words and phrases in that they are part of what Biber (1998) refers to as relatively "involved" rather than "informational" speech... What Biber labels as "involved" is one's self as an evaluating and emotional entity. (Moore 2005, 358–59)

A Chinese *Ku* person is supposed to be willfully individualistic, tough, and emotionally controlled. Emerging from a collective culture, the political implication of this character type is unmistakable. Characters from Wang Shuo's stories, mischievous tongue-in-cheek hooligans, for example, can well be an illustration of *Ku* rebels. Rock'n'roll, a rebel category in the Chinese contemporary music scene, is the emotive pulse of Generation *Ku*: "a cultural complex from the American 1960s was incorporated as a whole to the rock music scene of urban China in the 1990s" (Moore 2005, 362). *Ku* imagery is also a marketing tool, promoting fashion, food, and consumer goods important to Generation *Ku*. Social media use *Ku* concepts to attract traffic; the character *ku* appeared in web page titles 1.5 million times according to a survey (Gong Changyu 2002).

In the new millennium, a new "identity imaginary" cut into the public discourse; the year 2001 was considered by many as the year of *xiaozi* (petty bourgeoisie), when *xiaozi* publications—newspaper columns and journal series—mushroomed (Zheng Jian 2008). *Xiaozi* culture successfully created a space in the culture for with which its members identified, and it co-existed with such other cultural layers as "main melody" (ideological mainstream), intellectual élite culture, mischievous hooliganism (e.g., shown in Wang Shuo-style cultural artifacts), *kuso* entertainment (e.g., shown in Stephen Chow-style films), and mass culture. Ideologically, *xiaozi* believes in individualism (one needs to work hard to be successful) and humanism (let love reign our world—*"renjian da ai"*). These beliefs, nonetheless, are not supposed to be discussed philosophically according to the *xiaozi* way of life. Primarily seen as a lifestyle and sensibility, *xiaozi* embody their vague beliefs in things they enjoy doing, films they watch, books they read, or music they listen to. A list of these can contain films by Wong Kaiwai, stories by Aileen Zhang, novels by Haruki Murakami, Jazz or New Age music, sitting at a bar or riding in subway: values communicated not through concepts, but through styles, tastes, and codes.

Analyzing a literary work, critic Li Tuo writes, "Moonlight Sonata, Lorca's poems, snow-white skirt, black tea and red wine—these are codes that even today's *xiaozi* are still sharing and using to find each other" (Li Yunlei 2013, 41). A member of the *xiaozi,* as I have written elsewhere, "cares about styles, follows fashions, is particular about brand names, emphasizes aesthetic taste, nourishes sentiments, searches romance, loves the aura of the metropolis, travels in cyberspace" (Kuoshu 2011, 15).

A contemporary of *xiaozi* culture, *wulitou* is still another cultural fad that appears very much like Generation *Ku's* Wang Shuo, with his hooligans and endless mockery, re-packaged linguistically from Beijing street slang to Cantonese dialect. *Wulitou*, literally, "not seeing where it's coming from," is Cantonese slang referring to un-expectedness and nonsense. It denotes a style of forcing connections between things and events that are originally not connected to achieve a hilarious effect. To many, the boiling point of the feverish *wulitou* culture was 1996 when screenings of Hong Kong comedian Stephen Chow's *A Chinese Odyssey* became carnival events on Chinese college campuses. Students watched the film time and again, could recite dialogues from it, and could clone them into their real-life situations (Yin Kangzhuang 2010). What captured the Chinese college imagination was a fresh rhetoric of defiance, exaggeration, sarcasms, and occasional self-mockery. Publications, such as *Treasured Dictionary on a Chinese Odyssey* (Da hua xiyou baodian, 2000) and *An Incomplete Handbook on Stephen Chow* (Zhou Xingchi buwanquan shouce, 2000), aided the carnival, as did Stephen Chow's visit to Beijing University in 2001. The rebellious thrust of *wulitou* captured people with bewilderment. "What dreamed by intellectuals to deconstruct all," a commentator on Stephen Chow writes, "was achieved by master Chow without much effort" (Yin Kangzhuang 2010, 21). From this point on, *wulitou* literature boomed. In 2002 Chinese Cinema Press published an anthology collecting all sorts of *wulitou*-style writings. Between 2002 and 2003, *Guangzhou Arts and Literature* journal (*Guangzhou wenyi*) featured several special issues on *wulitou* campus literature. The year 2004 was a big year when several *wulitou*-style books were published, such as *Sha Monk's Diary, Run, Baoyu, Run,* and *Fake Jin Yong.* "With its fountainhead in Hong Kong," a Chinese scholar observes, "*wulitou* was re-casted in mainland, becoming a vehicle and channel for the young people to express their innermost feelings and to understand their own lives" (Yin Kangzhuang 2010, 22). In the *wulitou* entry of the Chinese online encyclopedia *Baidu baike*, an anonymous author posts three questions for its readers to test if they have lived like a *wulitou* person that day: Is your self-consciousness strongly emphasized? Are being free and being happy your most prioritized goals? Do you know how to create joy for yourself?

While Generation *Ku*, *wulitou*, and *xiaozi* gained initial attention primarily in old-fashioned ways—through books, literary works, concerts, and films—the next trend, Generation Q, is the hybrid offspring of the internet and the globalized market culture, and it peaked in about 2005, when China's social media QQ claims a user increase from several dozens of thousands to ten million in a couple of years (Du Jinyan 2006). QQ, the social media initially known as ICQ (I Seek You), obviously lent this generation its name. ChinaNews.com listed three other sources that also helped give rise to the name: first, the adorable anime characters created by Japanese artist Tezuka Osamu, which depict serious characters as infant-like and become the core of Q-generation taste; second, the Japanese fad (especially for young women) of using "cute" or "Q" to replace "ka wai" (lovely); and third, a positive refiguring of Ah Q, a Chinese everyman from Lu Xun's short story who is good at conjuring "spiritual triumph" while encountering defeat in life. Inspired by images ranging from Japanese cartoon characters to a character from Chinese fiction, Q persons enjoy escapist roleplaying and cosplay (dressing in costume). Q persons are distinguished by their linguistically playful Q language (*Q yan Q yu*). Q language, resembling its contemporary, *wulitou,* tends to jeer at traditional heroes and enjoys recreating B-type characters in all sorts of Q-version online literature. In 2004, a Q-version Chinese textbook published in Yunnan became a national hit. Literary scholar Tao Dongfeng sees the role of this textbook as spreading *wulitou* style in mainland China and producing a popular "mass culture text":

> It uses parody, collage, mixing, juxtaposition, and confusion of time and locations to jeer at and to undermine the mainstream order of discourses as well as the aesthetics, ethics and ideology that back up this order. (Tao Dongfeng et al. 2005, 51)

Confirming their rebellious role, Tao also explains that light-hearted Q followers typically express a mentality that rejects being constructive, as testified by the author of this textbook that he "only wants to be a happy person" and he "never thinks of replacing the others" (Tao Dongfeng et al. 2005, 53). Tao applauds the Q rebels but also worries that they bring about negative cynicism that may cause general social decay. This Q

Chinese textbook eventually touched the sensitive nerves of the sensors and got banned. Considering its social effects, Q culture is not just confined to youth. Role-playing is crucial for being cute; one does not necessarily need to be extremely young to be cute since he can always pretend to be young. To be cute for many is to find a psychological shelter from tension caused by modern rhythm of life. People of all age groups in today's China, in different degrees, show traces of Q language when they do online or phone messaging.

Although trends in youth culture have been influential in Chinese contemporary life, the Chinese scholarly consensus is that they are subcultures, that is, they affect only a small portion of the population, and their social impact should not be overstated. The critical consensus of *Crazy Stone*, however, is that it is a film of the grassroots, and it appeals to the grassroots. Grassroots, obviously, refers not just to a small portion of the population. How does Ning Hao, twenty-nine years old, when he directed *Crazy Stone*, bridge youth culture and the culture of the grassroots? In this context, Zhang Yiwu's assertion of *hou xiaozi* becomes meaningful, since it can answer our question from several perspectives. First, the composition of the masses needs to be refigured. The major components of the masses are not the illiterate working poor of the old days but a population that is becoming somewhat educated, online literate, and more involved. The grassroots today consist of, as Zhang puts it, "a large community produced by the internet and a huge mass of population centered on the youth" (Zheng Dongtian et al. 2006, 16). Second, *wulitou* persons, Q persons, and *xiaozi* are often more of a representational identity than a social and economic status. In real life, the majority of these young people are actually being pushed to the bottom of society in the process of social polarization. Their conditions, for example, are depicted by such Chinese books as *Ants Tribes* and *Working Bees* (Li Yunlei 2013, 39).[4] Their low social status allows them not only to understand the needs of the masses but also to become members of the masses. Third, *xiaozi* has a historical tradition in China of being independent from political dictatorship and ideological indoctrination. *Xiaozi* in recent Chinese history, as a leading scholar points out, often refers to "intellectuals who hold the beliefs in equality, freedom and love, who are somewhat independent politically, and who are *avant garde* in arts" (He Ping et al. 2005, 52). Fourth, *xiaozi* translates better to the masses. "*Xiaozi* culture," as Li Yunlei points out, "is a media between élite culture and mass culture. Messages of élite culture are often too vague and difficult for the masses to accept. They need to be represented in some simple, effective signs so that they can widely circulate in the society. Here enters the importance of *xiaozi* culture" (Li Yunlei 2013, 41). A distinguished literary critic, Li Tuo, would even claim that *xiaozi* is playing a leadership role in today's China, as entire Chinese cultural characteristics are becoming more and more *xiaozi* (Li Yunlei 2013, 39).

3   CARNIVAL

The popularity of Russian philosopher M. M. Bakhtin's ideas on carnival gained momentum in China with the introduction of American scholar John Fiske's theory of popular culture. Discussed primarily in the books *Problems of Dostoevsky's Poetics* and *Rabelais and His Worlds*, Bakhtin's carnival theory subverts and liberates the assumptions of dominant literary worlds through comic violence, bad language, exaggeration, satire, and shape-shifting, which are elements found in the medieval European carnivals. The carnival theory, as Benzi Zhang (1999, 19) from Chinese University of Hong Kong points out, "presents a vision of literature as comprising various carnivalizing forces in a process of constant shifts and movements that confront a totalizing center." He believes that the theory embodies Bakhtin's most democratic vision of "non-hierarchical plural systems" applicable to both literature and culture, and he calls for a necessary "carnivalistic mode of *(un)thinking* that accommodates rather than reduces the variety of literary and cultural manifestations from a 'monologic position'" (20). Bakhtin's impact in China had been fairly substantial. In addition to separate titles of translation of his books, his complete works were translated by Qian Zhongwen and published in seven volumes in 1998. Three years later, in 2001, two of Fiske's influential books, *Understanding Popular Culture* and *Reading the Popular*, were published in Chinese. In 2002 and 2003, Beijing Normal University professor Lu Daofu published two articles introducing Fiske in relation to Bakhtin, particularly to his carnival theory.[5] Surveying Chinese leading scholars' introductory work on Fiske, Lu also offers his own assessment of how the core of Bakhtin's carnival theory is represented by such key concepts as the populace, the ritual, the equality, and the subversion, as well as how Fiske has creatively used Bakhtin's carnival theory to explain a phenomenon of popular culture in the West, the craze for WWE wrestling on TV, which can be seen as a carnival of bodies, rule-breaking, grotesquerie, degradation, and even depoliticization of official ideology.

Concerning this Western way of helping the Chinese to apply Bakhtin to cultural analysis, one Chinese scholar (Zeng Jun 2006) points out that the Chinese are busy accessing Bakhtin in other ways: via the Russian discourse of traditional Marxism, for example, and the Western understanding of Bakhtin in the post-era (e.g., post-structuralist, postmodern, and post-colonial). In this "polyphony of Chinese reception of Bakhtin," which is the title of this author's 2004 book, there also emerges, most noticeably, a changed take on popular culture: a turn from modernist disdain of popular culture to the postmodern removal of cultural hierarchy and its understanding of the need for added analysis of popular culture. Fiske's use of Barkhtin's carnival theory illustrates not only this modern/postmodern shift but also the shift of Western scholarly Marxism from Frankfurt School traditions to the new interpretations offered by scholars of the Birmingham School. "The liberating function expected by Frankfurt scholars of the élite culture," Zeng writes, "is deconstructed and in its place is found the resistance of popular culture as represented by youth subcultures" (Zeng Jun 2006, 4).

Owing to this particularly oriented introduction of Bakhtin's carnival theory in relation to the studies of popular culture, before the black carnival induced by *Crazy Stone*, a major branch of articles on Barkhtin in China used his carnival theory to explain elements of Chinese popular culture such as mass media, phone messaging, and internet entertainment. When *Crazy Stone* arrived, "carnival" had become a trendy and popular phrase showing up frequently in the discourse about this film. The film, for example, is often described as a feast of fools. The absurdity of the characters and the eruption of their normally suppressed voices and energy are believed to showcase "a carnival of human nature being twisted and suppressed to become abnormal." This carnival reflects their being "marginalized in life" and their struggle caused by having fallen into the cultural "cracks" (zones of tension) in the emerging Chinese metropolis; their rebellion is also just their "unsettlement in life" (Gong Jie 2007, 33). When this film critic points out the lack of distinction between the thieves and the protectors of the treasured stone (because of their equal, marginalized status), I am sure he has pointed out a Bakhtin element of carnival, that is, the carnivalistic misalliance. Another element of carnival, the use of rituals, is also picked up by film reviewers to express a similar reading of the film as a depiction of the Chinese lost in confusion about their cultural orientation. "Carnival Rituals of Liminality" (Zhu Maoqing 2007), one review of *Crazy Stone*, refers to the anthropological concept of liminality proposed by Arnold van Gennep. In Gennep's framework, liminality indicates ambiguity and disorientation that occurs in a middle stage of rituals when participants become anonymous—no longer holding their pre-ritual status but having not yet begun the transition to the status they will hold in their post-ritual life. This anonymous status is called carnival because this "at-the-threshold" cultural experience will often reverse or temporarily dissolve social hierarchies, question continuity of tradition, and become uncertain about the future.

Crazy Stone's carnival is also constituted linguistically by casting the richly diversified Chinese dialects. The film features comic dialogues of these dialects and of Chinese intermingled with English. This element of comedy reflects the biggest migration and cultural relocation of Chinese in recent history. The demography of all Chinese cities has been rewritten, and all these cities are nourishing the new culture of a more complex social hierarchy concerning the locals and the migrants. Just as dialects can reflect social hierarchy, the use of English can also indicate a map of cultural traffic. The use of English in the film is sarcastic, in the same vein as petty thieves in the film bragging about professionalism. The craziness of this kind of English, profane and related with mannerisms, is a far cry from the "Crazy English" of Zhang Yuan's 1999 documentary film of the same title, which records China's popular frenzy to learn English and how this craze for English is given a nationalist bent: "Conquer English to Make China Stronger!" About a decade later, on the eve of China hosting the Olympics, *The New Yorker*'s Evan Osnos (2008) was still impressed by this linguistic passion:

> China today is divided by class, opportunity, and power, but one of its few unifying beliefs—something shared by waiters, politicians, intellectuals, tycoons—is the power of English ... English has become an ideology, a force strong enough to remake your résumé, attract a spouse, or catapult you out of a village.

Crazy Stone's crazy English users recall this myth by rendering it comical. As true to the nature of a carnival, opposites such as truth and fantasy are mingled, and the ready-made truths of myths and slogans are profaned and overturned.

4   *EGAO* (MISCHIEVOUS PARODY)
AND *SHANZHAI* (COPYCATTING)

Stylistically, *Crazy Stone* is noted for its mischievous parody, which in Chinese is known as *egao* (in the spirit of the term, if you say "egg owl," you have said it closely enough). *Egao* started in China first as a fad in the internet gaming community, where Photoshop software enabled fans to play with images and icons to comic effect. The resulting images—memes—can feature either celebrities or more obscure people, such as those caricaturized in the "chubby" (xiao pangzi) series or "indecent men" (weisuo nan) series. The humor stemming from these jokes is often a mixture of mockery and self-mockery. In this context, thinking of French-American painter Marcel Duchamp's classical parody "L.H.O.O.Q" (Mona Lisa with a mustache) is helpful in getting a sense of what *egao* is like. When the whole of China was clouded by the SARS outbreak, for example, the internet featured a flash video, showing chicks, suggesting migrant countryside girls, singing; "the same chicken meat, the same eggs, and the same us; how is it that we have turned into the source of a plague?!" Many sensing the pain of social inequality can read this unhappiness into these singing chicks.

Although *kuso*, a similar fad in the Japanese gaming community, is often considered a source of inspiration for Chinese *egao*, a more important inspiration, as it concerns *Crazy Stone* and other film production, are the films of Hong Kong comedian Stephen Chow and related *wulitou* humor. With over fifty titles to his credit, Stephen Chow challenges the established icons (think of his Monkey King and the Tang dynasty monk Tripikata); jeers at things that are usually solemn, distinguished, and respected; and portrays grassroots anti-heroes "heroically." His characters often cherish their petty dreams and dignity in the awkwardness of their trivial lives; their wishes and difficulties in becoming heroic often mock traditional heroism. "The game-like narrative and the mischievous carnival" found in Stephen Chow's films, writes Chinese scholar Wang Li, "deeply influenced a generation of Chinese youth on high school and college campuses, impacted other layers of the society as well, and prepared the emergence of Chinese *egao*" (Wang Li 2009, 228).

The most prominent event in Chinese *egao* history was the uploading of "*Yige mantou yinfa de xuean*" ("A bloody case all caused by a bun"), a short video created by Hu Ge in 2005, to mock Chen Kaige's film *The Promise* (Wuji, 2005). The twenty-odd-minute-long video triggered heated responses and a whirlwind of downloading, apparently set off by general dissatisfaction with big-budget Chinese films (*The Promise* cost more than 300 million RMB to produce). The event also induced more *egao* creations satirizing established artistic works. These *egao* films often achieve their hilarious effects by editing well-known footage of the targeted works into their own storylines, often with new soundtracks that totally violate the originals.

Crazy Stone relies on *egao* parody to engage the audience and to generate intertextual, often sarcastic, associations. Watching the film, the audience is constantly reminded of various moments of popular Western and Chinese films as well as many popular entertainment shows. Ning Hao's arrangements of dropping things from great heights, making use of sewage tunnels, and having both the thieves and the protectors of the jade live in the same building all recall the French comic film *La Grande Vadrouille* (1966), the Chinese-dubbed version of which was popular online. Filmgoers laugh when they see thieves dressed as Batman; the parody renders the thieves funny and mocks their anti-heroic character types. The rope use that is well known in the American *Mission Impossible* movies is also employed by the thief coming from Hong Kong in *Crazy Stone,* only to show how his "professionalism" is spoiled by the rope dealer; the shortened rope disrupts the whole rope-using plan (Fig. 3.1). The sarcasm with which the thieves constantly remind each other to be professional invokes the same feature of Feng Xiaogang's film *A World without Thieves* (2004).

Fig. 3.1   *Crazy Stone. Egao* (mischievous parody) reference to *Mission Impossible*

The use of flying daggers conjures Zhang Yimou's *House of Flying Daggers* (2004). A chase scene suggests Lu Chuan's *The Missing Gun* (2002). A dance scene imitates a most popular dance show, "Resourceful Bodhisattva" (*qianshou Guanyin*), from the 2005 Chinese CCTV New Year Gala. A character hums his own funny adaptation of the well-known song by popular singer Dao Lang, "The First Snow of 2002."

The implications of *egao*, it is interesting to note, are interpreted primarily in terms of postmodernism. First of all, it is about challenging authority and undermining its structured values. "*Egao*," as the Chinese web encyclopedia *Baidu Baike* describes it, "is ordinary folks' gesture of satirical deconstruction. *Egao* is a favored folk version of cultural criticism. *Egao* is folksy search for spirituality in a down-to-earth but fun manner." One should make a special note of the use of "deconstruction" here in relation to China's political culture. We should remember that in China Derrida has been hailed as *hou xiandai sixiang dashi* (postmodern master thinker), and postmodernism has had a respectable Chinese following. Yet, as several scholars have argued, Chinese versions of the postmodern, as compared with their Western predecessors, have a different relationship to modernity and modernism (Gao 2003, 247–48; McGrath 2008, 6). In China, postmodernity is not, as Frederic Jameson describes its Western predecessor, "the cultural logic of late capitalism" (Jameson 1991, 1). It is not a critique of modernity in late capitalism but a critique of modernity in late socialism (or post-socialism as the term currently goes). It is the cultural adjustment of imposing the dominance of the market on a socialist system. In one perspective, a significant part of the discourse on modernity in China has been monopolized and engineered by the Party to push for its post-Mao economic development. Thus it has become the continuation of the grand discourse ("grand logocentrism") of Maoist socialism, which becomes the target of criticism or ridicule by both the élite and popular cultures. Although *egao* represents popular culture's challenge to both political culture and élite culture, the élite culture continues to define *egao* in the positive light of postmodernist deconstruction, which is commonly understood more as a tearing down in the political sense.

Second, the feelings aroused by *egao* can be better understood in light of a particular aspect of postmodernism, that is, post-emotionalism. The term, coming from Stjepan Gabriel Meštrović's book *Postemotional Society* (1997), is about how humans are becoming more and more controlled by the cultural industry, not only their rational thinking but also their emotions (1997, 8). Post-emotionalism is interestingly applied to Chinese post-Mao cultural scenes by the Beijing-based scholar Wang Yichuan, who in his use of the term heeds more its role in cultural rebellions than to its role to control people. In making his argument, Wang first builds a sketchy trajectory of varied roles played by emotion in post-Mao China. In the 1970s, as a rejection of the over-politicization of Chinese literature and art in Maoist areas, a wave of emotionalism, along with the so-called internal turn (highlighting stream of consciousness and hidden emotions) and the emphasis on subjectivity, started to surge. This surge was part of the re-humanization efforts of the time and is meant for a more comprehensive re-engineering of human beings. Reality (to detach human beings from political artificiality and to restore them to their true complexity of emotions) was the aim and foundation of the surge. In the 1980s, foreign influences ranging from Gabriel Garcia Marquez's magic realism to Jameson's discussion of postmodern commercialization of emotion started to combine with the Chinese cultural identity crisis, which added layers of emotions that are not exactly based on immediate reality and resulted in such trends as primitivism, *avant-garde* representation, and postmodernist alienation from genuine emotions. Here, formalist experiments in the portrayal of emotions have prepared people for the emergence of post-emotionalism, which, as Wang Yichuan (2004, 7) explains, "is based on a new aesthetic conception that literature and arts can substitute, surrogate, rent or sell emotions."

Wang sees the indication of the arrival of post-emotionalism in the popularity enjoyed by writer Wang Shuo and filmmaker Feng Xiaogang, each of whom has a telling work in which emotions have become products of service—the emotional brokerage company in Wang Shuo's *Troubleshooters* and the dream fabricating company in Feng Xiaogang's *Party A & Party B*. For both artists, "topics favored by the élite culture of the 1980s, such as emotion, history, revolution and tradition, are all jeered at, showing a general playful and teasing attitude towards (genuine) emotions" (Wang Yichuan 2003, 16). The emotion in their works, Wang argues, "is a kind of virtual, imaginative one. It has characteristics of non-emotion and it is the result of teasing and cancelling the 'genuine emotions'" (Wang Yichuan 2003, 17). The popularity of these two plebian artists, as Wang Yichuan (2004) observes, is accompanied by the development of a new type of cultural industry in China that relies on a light-hearted gaming outlook and produces emotional products in large quantities according to the aesthetics of post-emotionalism. It appears that the Chinese are adjusting themselves for the transition from "devoted emotional gazes" (emotionalism) to "fleeting looks" at dazzling visual pieces in quick motion (post-emotionalism) (Wang Yichuan 2004, 8). China is heading into a post-emotionalist society, in which Meštrović's term the "ethic of niceness" rules—it does not matter if emotions are imagined, only possible in a virtual world, or are packaged for sale as long as they make one feel nice. *Egao* further testifies to the existence of post-emotionalism in China. To create comic absurdity, *egao* teases many emotive moments from established, popular works. Part of its goal is to keep its audience non-involved with those emotions it ridicules. This goal is very much the same as the alienation effect used by German dramatist Brecht, which aims at keeping the audience members as non-involved onlookers.

Third, in a narrowed-down and much exaggerated form, *egao* illustrates a major characteristic of postmodernism, that is, intertextuality. Tiphane Samoyault's book *L'intertextualité* was translated into Chinese in 2003 and became influential. Referring to the wide range of intertextual relations discussed in this book, such as citation, allusion, reference, pastiche, parody, and plagiary, some scholars claim that postmodernism uses intertextuality to demystify the uniqueness of any text, and in doing so, "there is seriousness behind game-like strategies and there is expectation of rebuilding in the effort of tearing down" (Chen Linxia 2006, 37). Confirming the cultural significance of *egao*, these scholars also worry about its mass culture characteristics that polarize between violent confrontation and escapism and how these characteristics may lead Chinese culture into nihilism (Chen Linxia 2006).

Fourth, *egao* testifies to a hybrid Chinese audience. IN-BETWEEN is where *egao* leads its audience to be. From this perspective, the human behaviors on and in front of the screen, especially in their interplay, constitute a process of becoming. This interplay explains the Deleuzian concept of "rhizome" in a rhizomatic interaction of heterogeneous media; the interaction may produce a new story and a complex reception of it. According to Deleuze, entering this rhizomatic dynamic posits the spectator in-between. Retrieving multiple artistic elements of images, metaphors, moods, rhythms, tones, or aura, especially considering that they are between cultures and elapse in time, both the story and the reception of the story are in genesis with multiple possibilities. This uncertainty, multiplicity, and fluidity obviously also speak of the subjectivity in genesis.

Crazy Stone is also attributed to having given rise to the production of *shanzhai* films. The word *shangzhai*, literally a "mountain stronghold" for bandits, originally referred to small IT manufacturers selling less expensive products by echoing big brand names (such as hi-phone for iPhone) but soon evolved to mean a much broader imitation of cultural icons, fashions, and works (such as a *shanzhai* replica of Jay Chou or a *shanzhai* version of the official CCTV Chinese New Year Gala).[6] Just as in an earlier time Wang Shuo used the Maoist official discourse as a playground for imitation and ridicule, *shanzhai* culture is turning contemporary materialist culture into its playground. Although there are severe criticisms in China of *shanzhai*, of its invasion of copyrights and of its disruption of the market, there is also an abundance of observation that *shanzhai* is economically anti-monopoly, stylistically sarcastic, and culturally meeting the needs and amusement of the common folk. The year 2008 is remembered as the year of *shanzhai* when Google listed *shanzhai* (copycatting) as their top pick of China's new hot words. In December of 2008, China's official TV channel, CCTV, featured special coverage on *shanzhai*, claiming that it had turned from a commercial strategy to the most popular cultural phenomenon in China. The year 2008 also saw an online survey conducted by *China Youth* newspaper about *shanzhai*, in which the top five words of association offered by Chinese youth were grassroots, copying, renewal, DIY (do-it-yourself), and to fake a brand. These words show how *shanzhai* tickles young minds in China. The year 2008 happens to be the year when the impact of *Crazy Stone* was at its height, and such films as *Happy* and *Almost Perfect* were believed to have joined hands with *Crazy Stone* to have opened the road for *shanzhai* film to develop.

Referring to a subculture, people may be rather undecided about when to use *egao* and when to use *shanzhai* since the terms often lead to the same cultural products and phenomena. If we use *egao* to emphasize style and *shanzhai* to stress production, we then notice that *shanzhai* has added interesting topics of discourse in relation to the issue of *Crazy Stone* and the market. The popularity of *Crazy Stone* and a circle of films inspired by it draw reviewers' attention to the box office miracles these small- and medium-budget films produced. The reasons that these films, often less refined artistically and low-tech in production, can get audiences so excited despite a Chinese film market overwhelmingly dominated by high-budget and imported films, they believe, are their grassroots connection since these films understand the general public, and their mischievous parodies often help such an audience to vent their anxieties. Although the small- and medium-budget-film category to which *shanzhai* films belong accounts for only 10 percent of the Chinese film market, critics believe

Shanzhai films are functioning as indicators of how to break the doldrums of the Chinese film market.

Shanzhai is related to the making of popular culture in China. Here we see Fiske's impact: the new edition of his *Understanding Popular Culture* was published in China in 2006 as a title within the postmodern book series. Based on Fiske, Chinese scholars emphasize the distinction between cultural products produced by the for-profit industry in the name of masses and mass participation in the making of their own culture. Li Lingling (2009) maintains that *shanzhai* becomes possible in the era of Web 2.0 when the internet platform had started to nourish the culture of mass participation, and *shanzhai* reflects mass resistance to the mainstream culture. Chen Dianlin (2009) emphasizes that the production of *Shanzhai* films remains the for-profit pursuit of small venture capitalists targeting the masses as consumers. However, he also maintains that mass participation can easily be shown in the discourse and social interaction provoked by *shanzhai* films. Li Xiaofei relates *shangzhai* culture, consumerism, and the development of mass culture and points out its ideological implication:

> Chinese mass culture develops side by side with China's economic take-off. In a certain sense, it shows as an expansion of both the principles of consumerism and the profane hedonism. It also shows as the victory of the ideology of every-day life, reducing the impact of sublimity of the mainstream culture and its spiritual norms. (Li Xiaofei 2009, 125)

Seeing *shanzhai* films guided by this ideology, critics also widely acknowledge their lack of lasting impacts—these films are often quickly forgotten, even while they break box office records, by hitting on a fleeting concern of the time (Li Huoxiu 2010).

NOTES

1. Among the early articles are Dong Dingshan (1980) and Yuan Kejia (1982).
2. See, for example, Chen Xiaoming (1993), Zhang Yiwu (1993), and Wang Ning (1993).
3. Books by and on Pierre Bourdieu (1930–2002), the French sociologist, anthropologist, and philosopher, are readily available in Chinese translations.
4. *Yizu* (Ants tribes, 2009, Guangxi shifan daxue chubanshe) and *Gongfeng* (Working bees, 2012, Zhongxin chubanshe), both written by Beijing-based author Si Lian, investigate difficulties in life encountered by contemporary

university graduates, who in turn use these book titles to identify themselves as "the dislocated youth".

5. See Lu Daofu (2002) and (2003). Lu's first article appears in a special issue of *Waiguo wenxue yanjiu* (Foreign literature research) devoted to the study of Bakhtin, which features seven articles in total.

6. Known as "the pop-king of Asia," Jay Chou is a Taiwanese musician, singer-songwriter, music and film producer, actor, and director. Noted in Guinness World Records for its length, the number of performers involved, and the large size of its viewership, CCTV Chinese New Year Gala has been one of the most anticipated TV events in China since the mid-1980s.

References

Chinese Language Sources

Chen Dianlin. 2009. Shanzhai wenhua: dikang yu yiyu (Shanzhai Culture: Resistance and Ridicule). *Xueshu tansuo* (Academic Exploration) 1: 107–110.

Chen Linxia. 2006. Egao de xiju: dangxia dianying yishu de shangyehua silu yu xianjing (*Egao* Comedy: Orientations and Traps in Commercialization of Contemporary Film Arts). *Qilu yiyuan* (Journal of Shandong Arts Academy) 6: 37–42.

Chen Xi. 2011. Shilun dangdai yujing xia houxiandai hese youmo xiju de xushi celue (On Narratives of Post-Modern, Black-Humor Comedies in Contemporary Discourses). *Dianying pingjie* (Movie Reviews) 12: 1–3.

Chen Xiaoming. 1993. *Wubian de tiaozhan: Zhongguo xianfeng wenxue de houxiandai xing* (Borderless Challenge: The Postmodern Features of Chinese Avant-Garde Literature). Beijing: Beijing University Press.

Dong Dingshan. 1980. Suowei houxiandai pai xiaoshuo (The So-Called Postmodern Fiction). *Dushu* (Book Review) 12: 135–139.

Du Jinyan. 2006. Q ban: jiti moqi de ya wenhua (Q version: A Collectively-Agreed Subculture). *Qingnian yanjiu* (Youth Studies) 9: 10–15.

Gong Changyu. 2002. Ku wenhua mantan (Random Discussion of Ku Culture). *Daode yu wenming* (Ethics and Civilization) 2: 71–75.

Gong Jie. 2007. Houxiandai yujing xia de kuanghuan hua xushu (Carnival Narrative in the Discursive Context of Postmodernity). *Dianying pingjie* (Movie Review) 4: 33–34 and 37.

He Ping, et al. 2005. Dangxia wenxue zhong de xiaozi qingdiao he zhongchan jieji quwei (Petty-Bourgeois Sensibility and Middle Class Taste in Contemporary Literature). *Wenyi pinglun* (Literature and Art Criticism) 6: 50–55.

Hong Xiaonan, and Li Yan. 2010. Houxiandai zhuyi dui zhongguo daxuesheng ku wenhua de yingxiang (Postmodern Impact on Chinese College Students'

Ku Culture). *Dalian ligong daxue xuebao* (Journal of Dalian University of Technology—Social Sciences Edition) 31 (2): 35–39.

Jameson, Fredric. 1991. *Postmodernism, or, The Cultural Logic of Late Capitalism.* Durham: Duke University Press.

Jiang Tianping, and Xia Yiqun. 2007. Huangdan de shengyan, hou xiandai de kuanghuan: lun 'fengkuang de shitou' de houxiandai tezheng (Absurd Banquet, Postmodern Carnival: On the Postmodern Characteristics of *Crazy Stone*). *Dangdai wentan* (Contemporary Literary Platform) 2: 149–151.

Li Huoxiu. 2010. Yiyi de queshi yu jiangou: xiaofei wenhua yujing xia zhongguo shanzhai dianying fazhan xianzhuang de fansi (Absence and Construct of Meanings: Reflection on Chinese *Shanzhai* Films in the Context of Commercial Culture). *Dangdai dianying* (Contemporary Cinema) 2: 155–158.

Li Lingling. 2009. Shanzhai wenhua: web2.0 shidai de caogen kuanghuan (*Shanzhai* Culture: Grassroots Carnival in the Era of Web2.0). *Xinwen jie* (News Media) 1: 108–110.

Li Xiaofei. 2009. Shanzhai wenhua de sikao (Contemplation of *Shanzhai* Culture). *Xinwen jie* (News Media) 2: 124–126.

Li Yunlei. 2013. Xin xiaozi de dichenghua yu wenhua lingdaoquan wenti (New Petty Bourgeoisie's Touch with Lower Depth and the Issue of Cultural Leadership). *Nanfang wentan* (Southern Literary Platform) 1: 39–41.

Liu Xueming. 2007. Dazhong wenhua yu houxiandaizhuyi de ronghe: jianxi fengkuang de shitou de hou xiandai zhuyi tezheng (The Merge of Mass Culture and Postmodernism: A Brief Analysis of Postmodern Features of *Crazy Stone*). *Dianying pingjie* (Movie Review) 6: 33–34.

Lu Daofu. 2002. Kuanghuan lilun yu yuehan feisike de dazhong wenhua yanjiu (Carnival Theory and John Fiske's Research on Popular Culture). *Waiguo wenxue yanjiu* (Foreign Literature Research) 4: 21–27 and 154.

———. 2003. Yuehan feisike dazhong wenhua lilun yanjiu shuping (A Survey of the Research on John Fiske's Popular Culture Theory). *Xueshu yanjiu* (Scholarly Research) 1: 100–104.

Tao Dongfeng, et al. 2005. Guanyu *Q ban yuwen* yu dahua wenhua xianxiang de taolun (A Discussion About *Q version Chinese* and *wulitou* Culture). *Dangdai wentan* (Contemporary Literary Platform) 3: 50–53.

Wang Li. 2009. Zhuolue mofang haishi chuangzaoxing jiegou: houxiandai zhuyi guanzhao xia de wangluo e'gao (Cheap Imitation or Creative Deconstruction: Internet *Egao* Considered in Postmodern Perspective). *Kejiao wenhui* (Science and Education Digest) 5: 228 and 233.

Wang Ning. 1993. *Duoyuan gongsheng de shidai* (An Era of Multiplicity). Beijing: Beijing daxue chubanshe.

Wang Yichuan. 2003. Zhongguo dianying de hou qinggan shidai: yingxiong qishi lu (Era of Post-Emotionalism in Chinese Film Production: Ideas Inspired by the Film *Hero*). *Dangdai dianying* (Contemporary Cinema) 2: 16–18.

————. 2004. Cong qinggan zhuyi dao hou qinggan zhuyi (From Emotionalism to Post-Emotionalism). *Wenyi zhengming* (Arts Forum) 1: 6–9.

Wang Yuechuan. 2001. Hou xiandai hou zhimin zhuyi zai zhongguo (Postmodern and Post-Colonialism in China). *Jiangsu xingzheng xueyuan xuebao* (Journal of Jiansu University of Administration) 1: 119–125, 136.

Yin Kangzhuang. 2010. Wulitou wenhua tanlun (Tentative Comment on *Wulitou* Culture). *Jinan xuebao* (Journal of Jinan University—Philosophy and Social Sciences Edition) 1: 20–26.

Yuan Kejia. 1982. Guanyu hou xiandai zhuyi sichao (About Postmodern Trend of Thinking). *Guowai shehui kexue* (Social Sciences Abroad) 11: 28–31.

Zeng Jun. 2006. Bahejin kuanghuan hua lilun yu xifang makesi zhuyi (Bakhtin's Carnival Theory and Western Marxism). *Xibei shida xuebao* (Journal of Northwest Normal University) 43 (5): 1–8.

Zhang Yiwu. 1993. *Zai bianyuan chu zhuisuo: Disan shijie wenhua yu dangdai zhongguo wenxue* (Marginal Inquiries: The Third World Culture and Contemporary Chinese Literature). Beijing: Beijing University Press.

Zheng Dongtian, et al. 2006. Xinzuo pingyi: *fengkuang de shitou* (Discussion of New Movies: On *Crazy Stone*). *Dangdai dianying* (Contemporary Cinema) 5: 15–20.

Zheng Dongtian. 2008. Yiqun zhongguo nianqing dianyingren yu yige waiguo zhizhe de shengjiao (The Spiritual Exchange Between a Group of Chinese Young People and a Foreign Wise Man). *Dangdai dianying* (Contemporary Cinema) 4: 4–6.

Zhu Maoqing. 2007. Yuxian zhuangtai xia de kuanghuan yishi (Carnival Rituals in the Liminal Status). *Dianying pinglun* (Movie Review) 10: 27–28.

ENGLISH LANGUAGE SOURCES

Bell, Daniel. 1976. *The Cultural Contradictions of Capitalism*. New York: Basic Books.

Gao, Minglu. 2003. Post-Utopian Avant-Garde Art in China. In *Postmodernism and the Postsocialist Condition: Politicized Art Under Late Socialism*, ed. Ales Erjavec. Berkeley: University of California Press.

Hooper, B. 1991. Chinese Youth: The Nineties Generation. *Current History* 90: 264–269.

Kuoshu, Harry. 2011. *Metro Movies: Cinematic Urbanism in Post-Mao China*. Carbondale/Edwardsville: Southern Illinois University Press.

Marr, D., and S. Rosen. 1998. Chinese and Vietnamese Youth in the 1990s. *The China Journal* 40: 145–172.

McGrath, Jason. 2008. *Postsocialist Modernity: Chinese Cinema, Literature, and Criticism in the Market Age*. Stanford: Stanford University Press.

Moore, Robert L. 2005. Generation *Ku*: Individualism and China's Millennial Youth. *Ethnology* 44 (4): 357–376.

Naremore, James. 1995–1996. American Film Noir: The History of an Idea. *Film Quarterly* 49 (2): 12–28.

Osno, Evan. 2008. *Crazy English*: The National Scramble to Learn a New Language Before the Olympics. Posted April 28, 2008. www.newyorker.com/magazine/2008/04/28/crazy-english. Accessed 15 Mar 2016.

Zhang, Benzi. 1999. Mapping Carnivalistic Discourse in Japanese American Writing. *MELUS (Multi-Ethnic Literature of the United States)* 24 (4): 19–40.

CHAPTER 4

Films: Because of *Crazy Stone*

Abstract This chapter uses seven films to illustrate a cycle of films produced owing to the impact of *Crazy Stone*. These films ride the tides of cultural fads, are conscious of the selling points in the market, and are collectively building the brand recognition of a round of neo-noir comedies. Among these films, the encounter of *Crazy Stone* and *My Own Swordsman* helps illustrate a cultural carnival of national scale. The shared elements of this encounter, generally described as a postmodernism that is filled with playful use of collage, pastiche, parody, and neo-noir mischief, are discovered to be more successful in a vague ancient setting which allows more freedom for the stories to be funnier and storytelling more game-like, just like the surprises found in a masquerade. This encounter also includes a Chinese director's adaptation of the Coen brothers' neo-noir debut *Blood Simple*.

Keywords Darkness • Brand recognition • Postmodernism • Carnival • Coen brothers • Neo-noir • *Blood Simple* • *Forrest Gump* • *West Side Story* • Idealism • MacGuffin • Hong Kong

Just as *Pulp Fiction* has produced a cycle of commercially successful films of similar noir styles in the West, *Crazy Stone*, relaying its influence, has produced an alternative cycle in China. The films in this cycle are

H. H. Kuoshu, *Craziness and Carnival in Neo-Noir Chinese Cinema*, Chinese Literature and Culture in the World, https://doi.org/10.1007/978-3-030-73081-9_4

obviously more than what I have selected here for sampling. These films ride the tides of cultural fads, are conscious of the selling points in the market, and are collectively building the brand recognition of a round of neo-noir comedies.

1   *LOST AND FOUND*: DARKNESS FOR SALE

In 2007, hoping to reproduce the success of *Crazy Stone*, several producers had their eyes fixed on a script based on Liu Zhenyun's novel *Lost and Found* (Wo jiao Liu Yuejin). Liu's popularity had been proven—Feng Xiaogang's 2003 film *Cell Phone* was based on his novel, and it was a big hit. Given his visibility in a Chinese platform dedicated to exploring new forms of collaboration and fresh business models across media boundaries, Liu's potential was not only about storytelling but also about story selling.[1] The subject of *Lost and Found*, the confrontation between an unethical real estate developer (rich and corrupt) and a member of the grassroots (poor but aspiring), was also strikingly similar to that of *Crazy Stone*. Liu Yuejin works as a cook at a construction site. Like the migrant workers he feeds, he ekes out an existence in metropolitan Beijing, suffering misery and humiliation. His wife has dumped him for another man. He never imagines a life full of adventure. All this changes overnight. One day, he is chosen by his boss, Yan, to be a fake alibi so that the boss can cheat his embittered wife over his own affair with an actress. His brief connection with this unethical real estate developer, however, turns his life into a torturous rollercoaster ride. His "acting" reward, along with all his savings, is stolen on his way to the bank. Also lost is an IOU (I owe you) from the man who has taken Liu's wife; Liu will get a vast sum after six years if he accepts the split, and there is only a couple of months left to wait. Desperately trying to find his stolen bag, he acquires another stolen handbag (belonging to Yan's alienated wife), which contains a flash drive storing damaging evidence of crimes committed by Yan as well as by a couple of high-ranking government officials whom Yan has bribed. This possession brings down upon Liu all the hired hands employed by both Yan and the officials—a private investigator, some mobsters, and others. In the end, the private investigator turns out to be a cop who saves Liu's neck.

The black humor of this story, according to the author, derives from a metaphorical contrast of lambs and wolves. Liu is a lamb to tumble into a crowd of wolves who, as the Chinese proverb goes, are "wolves clothed in lambskin," that is, wolves pretending to be kind in order to bite. The docile lambs, in contrast, always want to appear more powerful than they really are. The darkness is that of exposé, the pitiful mannerism of the lambs while they confront the wolves and while they are suffering causes fear within the audience of the wolves, that is, of the social and cultural damage done by unethical business deals and government corruption (Fig. 4.1).

With a marketable script and a small but decent five million RMB investment in hands, the producers had a recent award-winning director Ma Liwen signed to do the film.[2] Known for her minute depiction of emotional nuances of female characters in her first two films, Ma is generally considered an *auteur* director. Yet, Ma knew the terms for signing on. There was not much room for her to be an *auteur* for this film, since the script had been finalized. The film was designed to be a dark one, since the darkness shown in the novel has already proven popular, and was set for release around the Chinese New Year. Accordingly, Ma decided that her job was not to tinker with the script, but to execute the storytelling in a particular film language (Ma Liwen and Wu Guanping 2008). The style Ma chose for *Lost and Found* was a far cry from *Crazy Stone*. Multiple-storyline structure was rejected because of the script. *Crazy Stone*'s sense of game, inspired by *egao* and affecting all levels of story narration, was also opted out. The film is actually deadly serious and the story is told in earnest, though with a rollercoaster speed of twist and turns. The only person who is comic, mostly in dialogues, is Liu. This comic effect, understood by Ma as the scriptwriter's "cold humor," frequently leaves the

Fig. 4.1 *Lost and Found*. Darkness for sale

audience no room and no time to laugh either because the situation is too grim or the story is too scary. The darkness of the film, because of the film's realistic style, is also chokingly frightening. The showcasing of the mobsters, for example, is not like parodies of Hong Kong mobster films used by other contemporary *egao* films. It causes real fear. Although Liu's neck is finally saved by the cop disguised as a private investigator, which reinforces the government's role in upholding justice, the actor (Liu Hua) who plays the cop happens to play the head con man in *Crazy Stone*. This bit of casting is the only dramatic release in *Lost and Found* that counters tension and fear; alas, it also appears to be the film's biggest dose of sarcasm.[3] With this sarcasm, the film's happy ending also becomes an illusion: when Liu, joined by his girlfriend (indicating his regained masculinity), returns to his hometown and opens a popular restaurant, Yan's alienated wife tracks him down, and the film ends with a close-up of Liu's confused look indicating his fear that the whole experience may start all over again.

The popularity of *Lost and Found* comes partially from its quick-paced editing of the twisting-and-turning story. Aiming at commercial success, Ma Liwen had *The Bourne Identity* in mind as a model, and she wanted to create a strong sense of tension. One reviewer even reads a game-like feeling into the intensity of the film: the confusion of constant chasing and being chased is "all because of money and the hidden word written in the folded money is hate"—for your not having enough, for someone keeping you from it, and for something that may deprive you of it (Zhou Quanxin 2008, 22). The film, the reviewer believes, eventually produces a feeling of absurdity because of the senseless chasing,

> When everyone is drawn to chasing, the meaning of love, friendship and living is rendered hollow because of it ... Human spirituality [as the film attests to] becomes desert-like along with the rise of materialism ... The utopia of "modernization" collapses ... The mass culture is led into the "huge market" of "the metropolis." (Zhou Quanxin 2008, 22)

Worth noting is the reviewer's assertion of the bankruptcy of the Party-monopolized ideology of modernization (a call to increase the general welfare and to reconnect the country with the world), the fragmenting social effect of drastic urbanization, and the spiritual/ethical barrenness blamed on the dawning of early capitalism and money fetishism in China. With this reading, the reviewer relates *Lost and Found* with the carnival discourse initiated by *Crazy Stone*. In this discourse, the mass carnival means to deconstruct ideological utopias and to make room for the development of mass culture in an all-around secularization in the political sense and in a country booming with market economy.

The carnival discourse also features a theme of grassroots. Relating *Lost and Found* to *Crazy Stone* in their use of members from the grassroots as the protagonists, Li Yang sees the emergence of the third kind of narrative model for their representation within contemporary commercial films (Li Yang 2008). The first kind is the realistic portrayal with much sadness and pathos, such as Lu Xuechang's 2003 film *Cala, My Dog*. The second kind is the depiction in black humor, noted for humor mixed with sadness, as shown in Yang Yazhou's 1998 film *A Tree in the House*. Li describes the ideological effect of the first two narrative models:

> In those days, there was a warm expectation for the formation of "new middle class" and "the new rich," accompanied by the frequent senses of volatility and defeat because of this drastic social process ... The unstable middle class then needs the sympathy for members of the lower social stratus to confirm their self-identity. (Li Yang 2008, 54)

The third narrative model introduces a sense of game playing. In this model, many postmodern characteristics of contemporary Chinese urban life, such as fragmentation, instability, and the possibility to reproduce (such as the jade replica in *Crazy Stone* and copies of the flash drive in *Lost and Found*) contribute to the game-like absurdity of the stories. The absurdity, according to Li, is not peculiar to the social conditions of the grassroots. These protagonists are not the owners of the stories but the "selling points." These films, often featuring the confrontation between the rich and poor, are still meant for the rising Chinese middle class to watch: the game-like narration removes any realistic threats for these potential viewers seeking entertainment,

> The potential viewers may look down with some jeering or look up with some jealousy. There is no need for pathos and there is no call for fear. (Li Yang 2008, 55)

When *Lost and Found* first introduces Liu as the protagonist, he is juxtaposed with a series of medium shots showing crowds of migrant construction workers showing up from nowhere to take their lunch break. This haunting, surreal, and documentary-like footage relates the protagonist with the crowd and seems to call for exploring the lives of these people. This expectation, however, is mistaken; the film turns out not to be about the migrants at all. From this perspective, another *Lost and Found* reviewer affirms Li's idea that the lower-class protagonists are not the owners of their stories. Believing that an ideological contract of commercial films is already well formulated between film producers, distributers, and the audience, Hu argues that Chinese cinema is completing a broader cultural process of removing the concept of social class from popular entertainment (Hu Puzhong 2008). Liu's portrayal throughout the film is purposefully "privatized" to de-emphasize his class affiliation and to focus more on him being "a lonely individual" and "an entity of existentialism" (Hu Puzhong 2008, 56). In other words, he is not any different from all the others who are thrown into the struggle for existence in a society that is now governed by the social Darwinian rule of survival of the fittest—the film's underlying allegory of lambs versus wolves best illustrates this struggle and its philosophy. The detachment from social class exploration, Hu asserts, diverts people's attention from the polarization of rich and poor in today's China and its related unhealthy social structure of rich and poor outnumbering a meager middle class. Delving into such a social structure, commercial films show collectors' curiosity in presenting a panorama of diversified human responses to living in such a society without a firm value commitment. One should make a particular note of Hu's lack of value commitment since this Chinese story differs from the Hollywood formula of a lonely individual making it by overcoming difficulties. To make a film like this calls for value assertion. Liu had already accepted humiliation and his value assertion by tightly grasping that IOU. In the film, after he discovers the crimes recorded in the flash drive, it never seems to occur to him that he has a civic duty to do something about it rather than pursue mere self-protection. Hu takes this depiction as an indication of cynicism not only of the character but also of the author of the film. Cynicism, Hu believes, is a major hindrance to the healthy growth of Chinese film aesthetics. Cynicism, as I discussed elsewhere in this study, is also both the critique and component of contemporary post-socialist ideology in China.

2   STONE HITTING ON SWORDS: A POSTMODERN MASQUERADE

When Beijing University professor Zhang Yiwu accessed the popular appeal of *Crazy Stone*, he had in mind the TV series *My Own Swordsman* (Wulin waizhuan), which appeared several months earlier in 2006 as a low-budget dark horse. The program secured a prime-time slot with CCTV, held the young Chinese TV audience in a spell, and produced heated online discussions. A situation comedy set in ancient times (allegedly during the Ming dynasty, but it is nonspecific), *My Own Swordsman*, is generally believed to have demonstrated a strong postmodern appeal. A jouranl review (Luo Luo 2006, 11) following the series' premier observed,

> *My Own Swordsman* shows a strong postmodern tendency. It is good at using collage, sarcasm, and mischievous parody, caring neither the limit of time and location nor the restriction of subjects. It plays freely with dialects, jokes, games, advertisements, popular music, or any elements from mass media. With a skillful mastery of parody and sarcasm, it depicts contemporary mannerism and presents a caricature of folks living in lightness, that is, life without weight of ideals.

According to Zhang Yiwu, the postmodernism vividly revealed in *My Own Swordsman* and captivatingly reiterated by *Crazy Stone* testifies to the transition of postmodernism in China from an *avant-garde* style to a grass-roots mode of imagination with a touch of craziness. Relatedly, the understanding of the grassroots in China is also evolving from the old-fashioned peasants and laborers to what Zhang Yiwu chooses to call *hou xiaozi* (post petty bourgeois), the visual-culture-nourished and the internet-empowered masses of modern youth. Here is how Zhang Yiwu describes these *hou xiaozi*,

> They have fairly good education. They have a wide range of experience aided by internet and "disc-watching." Yet they are not the high-brow, literary youth. They have encountered enough bitterness and frustration in life due to set backs. They also nourish vague hopes while trying to be afloat in waves of life. They have similar tastes with *xiaozi* (petty bourgeoisie) years back but they constitute a much larger and complex social group. (Zheng Dongtian et al. 2006, 16)

Although *hou xiaozi* may refer primarily to younger people, to Zhang Yiwu, in the internet-connected society, this group plays a role similar to the working masses of the older days in traditional society because they formulate public opinions, and they shape popular taste.

The encounter of *Crazy Stone* and *My Own Swordsman* can be described as stones hitting on swords in a cultural carnival of national scale. Filmmakers who want to preserve the energy generated by this encounter know that the *hou xiaozi* audience is not calling for the end of their carnival yet, and they want craziness to continue. Although the shared elements of this encounter, generally described as a postmodernism that is filled with playful use of collage, pastiche, parody, and neo-noir mischief, rendered both ancient and modern subject matter with equal success, many also discovered that a vague ancient setting offered more freedom for the stories to be funnier and the storytelling more game-like, just like the surprises found in a masquerade. Consequentially, Bai Qiulin directed *The Second Best* (Tianxia di er, 2007) (Fig. 4.2).[4] Wang Yuelun directed *Almost Perfect* (Shiquan jiu mei, 2008), which is followed by its sequel *Panda Express* (Xiongmao daxia, 2009). Among the films inspired by *Crazy Stone*,

Fig. 4.2 *The Second Best.* An ancient-costume masquerade

these titles have proven to be more successful at the box office.[5] In 2009, following a three-year hiatus from filmmaking to focus on directing the opening ceremony for the Beijing Olympics, the established director Zhang Yimou surprised many by joining this trend of carnival and profanity with his *A Simple Noodle Story* (San qian pai'an jingqi, 2009). Although the fundamental inspiration is Coen brothers' neo-noir film *Blood Simple*, which Zhang watched over twenty years ago without any translation but with intuitive understanding, the inspiration of *My Own Swordsman* on Zhang is unmistakable since Zhang made sure that its scriptwriter and female lead played the same roles for his film.[6] A Chinese reviewer also compares Zhang's resorting to Coen Brothers to feature his particular style of *xi, nao, feng* (comic, noisy and crazy) in this film to Ning Hao resorting to Guy Ritchie to produce a sense of craziness in *Crazy Stone* (Chen Linxia 2010, 48).

The Second Best: *To Uncrown National Heroes*

In building *egao* (mischievous parody) connection with the cultural trends of the time, *The Second Best* whets the audience's appetite by showcasing trendy events or persons in an ancient-costume masquerade. While telling a Qing dynasty story of Song San, the bankrupt descendant of a declining martial art family once awarded "the number one under the sky," who hopes to pay off debt by regaining the family title, the film and its scenes of competition allow many trendy events and persons to become parts of the show: "the bloody bun" event referring to the widespread ridicule of Chen Kaige's film *The Promise*; the popularity of the rising star Li Yugang, a young man whose fame rests on performing the female lead of *Farewell My Concubine*; the ambiguous response to Sister Hibiscus (furong jiejie), who is a self-made, daring, but popular internet figure; and the interest in the so-called super girl phenomenon (chaoji nüsheng xianxiang), a rebellion of assertive and creative young women reacting against popstar-pretty expectations—and the list of references goes on and on, including *egao* parodies of more than twenty films, both Chinese and international.

Categorized as a fast-food film, *The Second Best* uses the ripple effects of internet-sustained current events to engage its audience. Nonetheless, *The Second Best* has also succeeded in organizing its *egao* reference according to such topics as China getting caught in the politics of East and West and whether China needs to be the leader in the global arena. Set in a general backdrop of China preparing to host the 2008 Olympics, the film's jeering portrayal of nationalism and its philistine proposal that it is safer not to be Number One may serve as a testimony of a Chinese scholar's observation that Chinese internet nationalism (obviously an expression of *hou xiaozi*) turned from a period of agitation in the 1990s, represented by the heated discourse following the publication of *China Can Say No*,[7] to a new period known as "moving away from extremisms" (Liu Zhongze 2013). A scholar synthesizes his contemporary discussion of internet nationalism to assert that the change is due to (1) a rising middle class in China that prefers a milder, more rational approach to international issues; (2) China's increasing international cooperation with foreign countries promotes a more comprehensive understanding of these countries and reduces the portrayal of them as pure enemies; and (3) the fast-growing economic power of China allows its netizens to look at international issues with more confidence and less agitation (Liu Zhongze 2013, 38).

To show its artistic and thematic arrangement of *egao* reference, *The Second Best* opens with one that is perhaps not widely familiar—the opening sequences of two of Zhang Yimou's films, *Raise the Red Lantern* (1991) and *Red Sorghum* (1987). It is a close-up of Song San saying to the camera that he will have to kill himself if others continue to force him to regain the family glory. Then, in cartoon, a caricature of the family saga running throughout Chinese history is fabricated to show that his grandfather's eminence is only one episode of many drastic and varied roles his ancestors have played. With this family saga as backdrop, in an arena where Japanese assassins confront a Qing imperial clan aided by Western advisors, the film portrays Song San's opportunist pursuit of the award, money, instead of the title. The parody is of Zhang Yimou's parody of his own film, *Raise the Red Lantern* of *Red Sorghum*, but the elements involved show significant changes. In *Red Sorghum*, one may detect the trendy elements of carnival of 2006. The film showcases the rebellious impulse, the crowning of a folk, alternative tradition, and the yearning for empowerment for not only individuals but also, more important, the nation. The roots searching of the time rests on the hope that China will be strong again and nationalism inspires rebels. *Raise the Red Lantern* presents a more somber Zhang Yimou, and the film is concerned less with the empowerment of the nation and more with the entrapment of the individual, particularly women, in the exploitive culture. There is deepened criticism of tradition, but there is also a sense of doom instead of the hope for nationalist resurge. Showing a desire for continuing the mischievous rebellion of Zhang's first film, the opening parody in *The Second Best* also absorbs changes contained in Zhang Yimou's own parody. This parody now becomes the backdrop of *The Second Best*, illustrating a critical, alienated mindset, indulging in mischief, making fun of nationalism.

As an illustration of the carnival discourse of the time, one reviewer (Wang Guojie 2009) of *The Second Best* praises the film for its thoughtful use of parodies, believing that its showcasing of a genuine anti-hero has best illustrated Bakhtin's description of crowning in a carnival,

> [H]e who is crowned is the antipode of a real king, a slave or a jester; this act, as it were, opens and sanctifies the inside-out world of carnival. In the ritual of crowning all aspects of the actual ceremony—the symbols of authority that are handed over to the newly crowned king and the clothing in which he is dressed—all become ambivalent and acquire a veneer of joyful relativity; they become almost stage props (although these are ritual stage props); their symbolic meaning becomes two-leveled (as real symbols of power, that is in the noncarnival world, they are single-leveled, absolute, heavy, and monolithically serious). (Bakhtin 1984, 124–125)

For the 2006 *Crazy Stone* carnival, films by Hong Kong director Stephen Chow have generally been believed to be a major source of inspiration. Comparing *The Second Best* with the Chow films, however, this reviewer believed that Chow is not rebellious enough, since most of Chow's films still assume a hero narrative, that is, the anti-heroes are often endowed with a special ability and eventually become heroes. *The Second Best*, in contrast, never encourages the expectation that the opportunist Song San and his equally opportunist lady friend will end up as heroes—they remain the crowned clowns of a carnival. A major idea that informs this reviewer and many others is the role of carnival in keeping the "myth making" from being reproduced. Mythmaking, literally *zao shen* (deity making) in Chinese, goes against the non-hierarchical, plural system contained in the carnival vision of a culture.

Almost Perfect: A Doomed Quest

Almost Perfect makes a game of embedding a traditional love story into a hybridity of what Ihab Hassan (1986, 506) calls "the mutant replication of genres, including parody, travesty, pastiche." The story involves a quest for a highly desirable object that also brings disaster upon whoever possesses it (Fig. 4.3). Desire is caused for two reasons: (1) the object is a

Fig. 4.3 *Almost Perfect*. A doomed quest

secret how-to book of magical carpentry that has produced wonders such as a rocking chair that can restore youth and a wooden bird that can fly people wherever they want to go; (2) it contains a map of an imperial tomb and treasure trove where the last owner of the book, Master Tang, is buried alive once his carpentry work is completed. At the start of the film, the possessor of this secret book, a disciple of Master Tang, engages everyone's attention: the crowned prince of the Ming dynasty is so fascinated with carpentry that he leaves the palace in disguise to search for him; Master Tang's daughter, wishing for a proper burial for her father, disguises herself as a man to search for him; a special agent appointed by the Emperor wants him for questioning about a theft; and the owner of a brothel locks him up once the value of the secret book is discovered. In this brothel, all the interested parties meet, especially the prince and Miss Tang, who fall in love. Soon everyone hits the road again in pursuit of the brothel owner and her lover, heading south as they follow the map in the book. In the south, on the property of a rich family, everyone meets again in a carnival atmosphere: the brothel owner and her lover are mistaken for artists hired from the capital city; the imperial agent is retained by the family for odd jobs; and the prince, with Miss Tang disguised as his maid, arrives to pay a formal visit to the family, having taken part in a local custom intended to secure their daughter a husband.

The confrontation of two styles used in portraying the love triangle makes *Almost Perfect* interesting. The portrayal of the romantic love between the prince and Miss Tang is highly invested. The actor and actress who portray them are icons in China of love, youth, and fashion. The theme song of their meeting, and for the whole film, *The Pear Flower Flagrance*, is by the hottest pop singer of the time, Chris Lee (Li Yuchun), whose picture made the cover of *Time* magazine in 2005 in its "annual celebration of the courageous, the gifted, the inspired and the inspiring." Miss Tang is blessed by the Cinderella myth—it is she, instead of the rich daughter, who can step into the wooden shoes carved by the prince. However, it is not just their romantic love that is jeered (referred to as forbidden, gay love like characters from *Brokeback Mountain*). The lyricism in the story world for this love is also constantly challenged by the carnival in the south (be aware that the south was long the barbarian's realm in the cultural map of ancient China). Filled with *egao* rhetoric, the hybridity of the southern carnival mocks contemporary Chinese cultural dilemmas and thus appears filled with vitality, in contrast to the detachment of the pale romantic love. The songs by Back Dorm Boys, particularly "Captain Pirate," cheer up this carnival. The fame of the duo testifies to cultural hybridity—their web stardom rests on their lip-syncing to songs by America's Backstreet Boys. "Part of their appeal" as a reporter of *The Seattle Times* (Lee 2006) observes, "is the sheer mismatch of two Chinese men wearing basketball jerseys swaying their heads while mouthing the lyrics to English pop songs." This kind of mismatch is so symptomatic of the story world of *Almost Perfect*, in which, for example, the *waijiao* (foreign instructors) are scolded for supporting the crown prince in studying carpentry instead of classics; and the rich daughter of the south loves Harry Potter.

The confrontation of styles in *Almost Perfect* reminds us of the similar stylistic confrontation found in the Yuan dynasty play *Dou E Yuan* (Injustice done to Dou E). In this four-act play, the lyricism of the female lead, the only singing role among others talking and miming, battles against fast-paced slapstick foolishness but is continually defeated by it. Only in the concluding act, aided by the nationalist ideology of justice and the power of the supernatural, does her lyricism eventually win. Denouncing the dark age of Mongol rule in China, lyricism here is bound to win. For *Almost Perfect*, it is a different story. What confronts romantic love is the contemporary ideology of multiplicity and a cultural landscape of hybridity where cross-cultural influences mingle, blend, and lay upon one another. The hybridization, as Ihab Hassan describes, is like a thresh-old culture:

> [It is] at once young and very old. Cliché and plagiarism ("playgiarism," Raymond Federman punned), parody and pastiche, pop and kitsch enrich *re*-presentation. In this view, image or replica may be as valid as its model (the *Quixote* of Borge's Pierre Menard), may even bring an "*augment d'être*." This makes for a different concept of tradition, one which continuity and discontinuity, high and low culture, mingle not to imitate but to expand the past in the present. In that plural present, all styles are dialectically available in an interplay between the Now and the Not Now, the Same and the Other. (506)

Although *Almost Perfect* is more about "present in the past," it corresponds to the threshold features Hassan describes here. It also affirms the plurality of the culture and the lack of clear distinction between the present and the past. It may well be the doom of the secret book that allows the Ming prince to ascend the throne, master the carpentry, but lose his romantic love. The doom, nonetheless, is also metaphorical of a cultural hybridity, which makes the prince's lack of loyalty (shown in his attraction to the southern daughter) not too horrible.

A Simple Noodle Story: *Bright-Color, Neo-noir Profanity*

There has been a general confusion about Zhang Yimou's indebtedness to the Coen brothers' neo-noir debut *Blood Simple*. Across the ocean in America and in China too, the reception for Zhang's adaptation did not go well. In America, the Cohn brothers' original has a 94 percent "freshness rating" on rottentomatoes.com, Zhang's adaptation receives only a disappointing 32 percent. In China, among many other criticisms, such as accusations that Zhang has produced a "super copycat film" (chaoji shanzhai pian), some reviewers can't comprehend the magic of *Blood Simple*'s story that Zhang had followed faithfully and paid dearly (thirty million RMB) to recast. The polemic reception, however, did not keep the film from succeeding at the box office. The internationally known director Zhang Yimou has been described in China as a "phenomenal figure." Indeed, no director can compare with him for having attracted that much heated polarity for his films, that many times. In retrospect, many of these controversial films became milestones indicating either undercurrents or emerging trends in Chinese filmmaking.

In this particular juncture, Zhang was adding heat to the fad created by the interplay between *Crazy Stone* and *My Own Swordsman*. The fad was known for its connection with the Chinese grassroots, helping the domestic market of small- or medium-budget films, nourishing a cultural appetite for noir stories, leaning toward sarcasm as well as profanity, and showing commercial awareness in selling films. Zhang sought to appeal to a mainstream audience (*dazhong* in Chinese), but the story he purchased was that of an independent film meant for a smaller, selective US audience (*xiaozhong* in Chinese). No wonder the most drastic change of his adaptation, as observed by Jonathan Evans, is that it makes every effort to "make causality more explicit" (2014, 292) and rather than recalling *Blood Simple* and similar independent films, it instead resembles commercial, Hollywood remakes of films from other countries—popularly known as "a less than respectable Hollywood commercial practice" (Evans 2014, 285).

The mismatch, nonetheless, offers us an interesting interface between a Chinese filmmaking fad that displays some noir features and an American neo-noir film. As frequently observed, noir films, be they traditional or neo, are often a compound genre of noir elements plus something else, for example, screwball comedies, crime thrillers, and so on.[8] Just as *Blood Simple* needs to be seen as a reworking of classical noir films, *A Simple Noodle Story* tests the neo-noir's ability to mix itself not only with such genres as crime thrillers or cartoonish comedies but also with such folk-entertainment elements as acrobatic shows, skits, and sitcoms.

The appeal of *Blood Simple* to Zhang Yimou lies in its underlying similarity to a recurring narrative pattern of the struggle against a restrictive culture seen in many of Zhang's earlier films. *Blood Simple* is a story about desire. The only woman in the film, Abby, may not be a traditional film noir femme fatale, but she connects and witnesses the desires of the three leading men: Ray wishes to live up to the faithfulness of his new-found love with Abby, the alienated wife of his boss; Marty, Abby's husband and Ray's bar-owner boss, seeks vengeance through the deaths of Ray and Abby; and Visser, Marty's cynical hired killer, is greedy for money and is driven to murder by the emotional vulnerability of the two other men. When darkness reigns throughout the film and all the men die, among the complex responses to this film is a sympathy for the doom of a potentially genuine love. Zhang's adaptation is faithful to the original. The story moves from Texas to an ancient Chinese mountain town, and it builds on the same sense of doom. The femme fatale wife of the abusive owner of the noodle shop takes a sympathetic but effeminate employee as her lover. The vengeful husband, in hiring a corrupt policeman to kill the lovers, gets himself killed by the policeman's thirst for more money. The policeman, to get money from the safe and to protect himself, kills not only the lover but also another employee.

To emphasize the role a restrictive culture plays in this doomed situation, in his general effort to make the causality explicit, Zhang asserts that the noodle shop owner is not only an abusive husband but also an exploitive employer who can afford to purchase protection from local officials. In this sense, the darkness shown in the film turns from a grotesque gaze into human nature to a denunciation of the reigning terror in which money motivates political power and police work like bandits. With this change, *A Simple Noodle Story* compares better with Zhang's earlier film *Ju Dou* (1990), his classic film of lovers confronting restrictive culture. Yet China has changed so much between the two films that they demonstrate drastically different artistic styles and epoch spirits. What accounts for the difference between the two stories, according to Zhang Yiwu, is the "postmodern" rendition of *A Simple Noodle Story*. "With this absurdist farce," Zhang Yiwu writes, "Zhang Yimou uses laughter to replace cultural retrospection and leads us into a 'postmodern' realm of superficial sarcasm and misalliance" (Zhang Yiwu 2010, 29). Zhang Yiwu's discussion of *A Simple Noodle Story*, in summary, is threefold. (1) The film refuses to dig into any depth of characterization or to focus on any set meaning, even when functioning as a critique. In doing so, it is a far cry from the immediate post-Mao cultural critique in name of roots searching, which informs the making of *Ju Dou*. In a moral relativism, *A Simple Noodle Story* refers more to issues related to the general human nature. (2) The global-scale economic crisis of 2009 urged Zhang Yimou to focus on China's domestic film market. His effort to connect with the broadest audience leads him more to adopt the fun-seeking mischief of contemporary mass culture. In this film, he combines two winning tickets: the vast provincially popular skit as well as sitcom represented by Zhao Benshan and a more internet-based fad of *My Own Swordsman*. The result is a showcase of folk culture and a grotesque comedy contained within a story of doom. (3) If *Ju Dou*'s Chinese-ness offers film viewers from the West an *other* for understanding the restrictive culture of traditional China, the *otherness* shown by *A Simple Noodle Story* is concerned instead with reflecting on human nature, which greatly reduces the nature of the film's *otherness* and the film's distance from its source of inspiration, *Blood Simple*.

A striking deflection shown in *A Simple Noodle Story* is how the bleak landscape of Texas is turned into a most colorful Chinese setting with computer-enhanced brown and orange striations in soil, and equally bold colors of the characters' folk costumes, making this Zhang Yimou film even more a "postmodern" mischief in showcasing darkness, a deviation from the grim black-and-white cinematography typical of a noir film (Fig. 4.4). One of the reasons for Zhang Yimou's use of bold colors in this film may well be traced to the start of his career when he played the male lead in Wu Tianming's 1987 film *Old Well*. Wu explained how they once thought of shooting the film in black and white to best depict the aridity and poverty of the mountain village as well as the villagers' tenacity and strength. Then they discovered that "the harsher the life was in a place, the more striking were the colors used by its residents" and that the "sharp contrast of colors is the reality of life in the Chinese countryside" (Kuoshu 2002, 235). From there the film's color scheme resembled the style of peasant painting. What Wu sought with the color contrast then would be exactly what a critic may say about *A Simple Noodle Story* now: to let film "appear both ancient and modern," only needing to use the trendy term of postmodern to update modern (Kuoshu 2002, 235). If such concepts as poverty, aridity, and tenacity are related to Wu's color scheme, darkness and doom would be what Zhang Yimou's similar color scheme helps to contrast. It is in this sense a Chinese reviewer talks about "a black-hole kind of fear and desperation" hidden behind this film, which strikes as a

Fig. 4.4 *A Simple Noodle Story*. Bright-color, neo-noir profanity

"thrilling comedy," a "fairy-tale-like" showcase of "existential hell," and a grotesque "blank space" opened up by color as well as stylistic contrasts (Chen Mo 2010, 36).

3   *HAPPY:* IDEALISM, FORMALISM, AND BITTER LAUGHTER

Forrest Gump's popularity in China casts a cross-cultural backdrop for our discussion of *Happy* (Gaoxing, 2009), a noir comedy inspired by *Crazy Stone*. The lead character of the American film (Zemeckis, 1994), known intimately in China as "Ah Gump" (Dear Gump), has become an icon in Chinese popular culture, standing for such characteristics as honesty, sincerity, persistence, and kindheartedness. This Chinese popularity contrasts with the film's original homeland fame, which was set in a context of redefining American values after the Cold War. Lance Morrow describes a void of the time: "The collapse of communism and the Soviet empire suddenly removed the dark moral counterweight by which Americans measured their own virtue" (Morrow 1992, 50). This void forced Americans to challenge their prior-to-the-void period smugness and to re-examine the defining ideas of the nation. Although the redefinition was greatly utilized by the new conservatives to promote their political agenda, the popularity of *Forrest Gump* had a broader base, and it was related to the prevailing desire for reasserting the American dream. In its popularity, *Forrest Gump* became a space of negotiation; "the wide-scale effort to 'redefine America,'" as Jennifer Wang (2000, 92) describes in the case of the film's reception, "is itself defined not by consensus but by conflict."

At the same time, the Chinese were dealing with a similar void or the loss of "moral counterweight": the Chinese government in the post-Cold War era could no longer use American imperialism as the number one enemy to rally its people and to cover up some of its own problems.[9] With the bankruptcy of the Party-engineered socialist ideology, there was a dire need to redefine what it means to lead a meaningful everyday life. As the Chinese imported American blockbuster films, *Forrest Gump* became a hit when it met this need. Forrest Gump, with his "box of chocolates" philosophy, provided the Chinese a down-to-earth example, however mythical, of succeeding in life without glossy words, which, in China, were often associated with the hyperbole of propaganda. Also similar to its reception in the United States, the popularity of *Forrest Gump* in China resonated with an anti-intellectualism that could be traced through such cultural fads as Wang Shuo's hooliganism, "pretty woman writers" who focused on the body to downgrade the brain, and the *egao* (mischievous parody) trend in filmmaking and web publishing. The popularity of *Forrest Gump* in China reflected China's own artistic concern for the grassroots. This concern was evident not only in the attention paid to the plight of people suffering under recent market-oriented social changes in many works in the nature of exposé, but also in an all-round playfulness that characterized a particular facet of Chinese contemporary popular culture.

Into this context enters the Chinese film director calling himself Ah Gump, who has produced and directed films since 2000 and has by now more than twenty titles to his credit.[10] Ah Gump is a cultural broker, openly claiming that his work is dictated by the box office. He assembles popular and successful elements of entertainment to make his films. Although he has often been jeered as a producer of trashy films, he would be proud to tell you that his films sell. Among the various types of films he has directed, such as suspense and thrillers, what makes him most worthy of the name Ah Gump is his 2009 film *Happy* (Fig. 4.5).

Happy is based on the novella written by Jia Pingwa. It celebrates the dream to fly harbored by a migrant worker Gao Xing. Known in his rural village for enjoying the fancy hobby of making his own airplane, Gao Xing

Fig. 4.5 *Happy.* Forrest Gump in China

comes to the city of Xi'an with his friend Wu Fu. They become trash recyclers and dream of making it in the big city. Gao Xing falls in love with a massage girl, who is also a rural migrant with hopes for a better life. Although Gao Xing has no money to compete with her customers, who pay for her service and try to buy her love, Gao Xing eventually wins her heart with the sincerity of his feelings and the sacrifice he is willing to make for her. What Ah Gump achieves in the adaptation is to turn Jia's slice-of-life realism into a *West Side Story*-type musical with dark humor and celebration, which even forced the established writer Jia Pingwa to admit that he needs to reconsider how to approach the subject of misery and hardship in his writing (Anon. 2010).

Watching *Happy*, a Western critic would definitely see the influence of *West Side Story* (Wise and Robbins, 1961). Parallels can be made between the two films: the subject matter of young people in a poor neighborhood in a big city; the use of singing and dancing to depict their lives and to portray their love. While a comparative study of this kind is surely worthwhile in leading to an educated understanding of East/West difference in representation, one wonders why Chinese critics and director Ah Gump himself have never mentioned this classic film (though they surely know it[11]) but have spoken instead of a variety of more recent influences on *Happy*. Among these, for example, are the Western films *Chicago* (Marshall, 2002) and *Moulin Rouge* (Luhrmann, 2001), a Japanese film *Memories of Matsuko* (Nakashima, 2006), and the Western rap music now performed by the band *Heisa* based in Xi'an, the film's locale.[12] Looking into how Ah Gump talks about these works, one realizes that he is thinking of them in terms of his audience: how his audience at any given time is particularly formulated, that is, which artistic effects of which works are still retained by the audience, how these works, in constant interplay, are weaved together in the culture, and how Ah Gump himself can best sell his film by probing the effects and affects of these influences. Knowing this, one starts to realize that East/West, a-pair-of-works model is indeed insufficient to decipher the implications of *Happy*.

Ah Gump's attention to the audience reminds me of Alfred Hitchcock's description of his relationship to his own audience. Writing to his scriptwriter Ernest Lehman about *North by Northwest*, Hitchcock mused,

> Ernie, do you realize what we are doing in this picture? The audience is like a giant organ that you and I are playing. At one moment we play this note and get this reaction, and then we play that chord and they react that way.

And someday we won't even have to make a movie—there'll be electrodes implanted in their brains, and we'll just press different buttons and they'll go "oooh" and "aaah" and we'll frighten them, and make them laugh. Won't that be wonderful? (Spoto 1984, 440)

Ah Gump's *Happy* best illustrates Hitchcock's fantasy of probing for the "oooh" and "aaah" spots in the brain of his audience. Here, since China's "disc-watching" generation (Zhang Yiwu 2002) audience retains multiple elements supplied by a booming and ill-regulated video market, these spots highlight not only the international components of this market but also the hybrid nature of the emerging subjectivity of the disc-watching generation.

The central thrust of Ah Gump's *Happy* illustrates Spinoza's concept of joy, that is, to be active is to enjoy life and to be joyful is to form adequate thoughts and to act. In the filmic realm of *Happy*, the desire for happiness focuses on a Chinese story. It nonetheless needs to reach out for a great diversity of international, artistic elements to create joy. Seeing joy in this light is important since it may help overcome the prejudice that optimism in popular culture is often an indicator of the shallowness of ideas. Ah Gump's inspiration to adapt the novella into a film comes from the author Jia Pingwa's epigraph on the title-page: "What I depict is a group of awkward folks who lead clean lives in a filthy place." In this epigraph lies a traditional Confucian and Buddhist contrast of the "muddy" world tainted by human materialism and the simple actions taken by some individuals to not only make a living but also to preserve their dignity. The action these folks take, their connection with others, and their claiming of the world is what Ah Gump wants to celebrate. "I worship this sense of joy," Ah Gump explains, "and take it as an existential condition filled with freedom … [This joy] turns misfortunes instantly into lighthearted jeering; [in this mood] there is nothing that you cannot achieve and there are only things that you fail to imagine" (Anon. 2010). Ah Gump wants this joy to be the core of the idealism and formalism of his film.[13]

Perceptions and experiences form *Happy*'s idealism. "The image," as Patricia Pisters states, "is not seen as a representation (an umbilical cord) but as a thought-provoking encounter" (21). In this sense, it is less important for the images of Ah Gump's migrants, the trash recyclers, and the massage girls, to be a truthful representation of them in their real lives and their harsh working conditions. What is more important is that they, while "dancing" along with varied international artistic elements that help bring them to life, provide thought-provoking encounters with values and cultures contained in these artistic elements. These encounters sustain a complex claim to representation for migrants in name of idealism and a questioning of what it means to be migrants in contemporary urban China. The idealism allows Ah Gump to ridicule the status quo as well as to peep into the future, when the migrants may live better in a changed society.

Featuring a love story of two migrants, a love for each other and not for the wealth the other possesses, the singing and dancing in *Happy* is a eulogy of love that despises money-worshiping. The irony that one frequently detects in these musical aspects is primarily due to the film's critique of society's lack of sympathy for and exploitation of the migrants. The idealism endorses humanism, but it also exposes the gritty living conditions of the migrants that can easily dampen their spirituality. The social allegory of *Happy* definitely recalls *West Side Story*, in which singing and dancing alludes to a territorial tension between young immigrants of different ethnic groups in the new world of opportunities. "God helps those who help themselves"—the American Dream materialized in territory reassignment then, and the American Dream comes to China via *Forrest Gump* now, indicating that persistence will eventually bring success. *Happy* echoes this belief in a dream of its own; its version of happiness is aided by some playfulness and mischief. In the musical sequence entitled "We're Happy Trash Kings," rural migrants and city kids confront each other, and the migrants win. In the conclusion of the film, Beethoven's "Ode to Joy" dominates the soundtrack when the trash king, Gao Xing, succeeds: his plane made of recycled materials soars high in the sky of Xi'an, and his flight earns him the money to bail out the girl he loves. As he and the girl sit in a rickshaw that also flies into the sky (a moment imitating the bicycle flight in *ET*), the soundtrack's "Ode to Joy" becomes a mischievous rap performance, and the screen reveals the film set that produces the illusion of the rickshaw flight. Illusory as this ending may be, idealism still inspires the audience as it resonates with Beethoven's melody.

The idealism in *Happy* conceals sadness caused by hardship, which is achieved by contrasting the two central characters, Gao Xing and Wu Fu. Like traditional complementing characters in an allegory, such as the monk and the monkey in *Journey to the West*, they depict human beings from different angles. Gao Xing becomes idealism *per se*; his remote-controlled electronic airplane not only becomes a metaphor used throughout the film to highlight his optimism, it also turns into an actual plane that he

builds and uses to realize his dream. Gao Xing, on the one hand, personifies human hope that can soar high. Wu Fu, on the other hand, becomes
the reminder of their low social status and harsh economic condition in a
society that is turning more materialistic. If Gao Xing represents will-
power, Wu Fu is carnal, depicted by the basic needs for food, shelter, and
security. Ah Gump purposefully uses Wu Fu's coarse manner and gross
appetite to remind the audience of the rough environment from which the
film's central characters have emerged. Here Ah Gump becomes rather
heavy-handed, creating two scenes in which Wu Fu vomits—not just dis-
creet dribbles but copious projectile vomiting. These scenes disgust his
audience but serve to build a quick sense of the character's crudity and
vent some anger generated by the film's story—at one point, a bad guy is
totally covered with Wu Fu's vomit (Lao Yang 2009). Looking into the
reasons for these scenes, one realizes that Ah Gump is not original here;
he copies. "The most popular bodily function in the movies these days,"
an online blogger writes about Western films, "isn't sex. It's vomiting"
(AP 2010). Indeed, along with sex and violence, vomiting is just another
bodily hyperbole in the film medium that may function the same, for
example, as the so-called body writing of some Chinese contemporary
writers. Although vomiting has become, as another online blogger (Billson
2010) phrases it, a "recurring movie motif" in Western film since the
1960s and may have lost its ability to shock, the Chinese audience's unfa-
miliarity with such tactics helps make both vomiting scenes stand out vividly in Ah Gump's film.

Happy's singing and dancing is composed in direct reference of the
Japanese film *Memories of Matsuko*, which is popular in China but has a
drastically different treatment of idealism. In Matsuko's biographical film,
her difficulties are caused primarily by psychological and existential problems rather than social ones. Idealism prompts her to carry on, only to be
met with disappointment, leading her to conclude that "life is totally
meaningless," and that she needs to be forgiven for simply being born. In
this film, song and dance function to show that idealism is the very reason
for disappointment: every child equipped with the idealism of wanting to
reach high into the sky to pick stars will experience constant let-downs,
and eventually she will be converted to "the God" (the truth) which
embodies all the miseries in life. To be with God is to accept that life is
painful in itself, and to indulge in fantasies of singing and dancing will only
lead to more pain in life. Although *Memories of Matsuko* is held to be a
model for *Happy*, the two films are drastically different in cultural

orientations. Respectively, they feature existential contemplation in a developed country and social critique in a developing country. In contrast, although *West Side Story* is not the declared model for *Happy*, the two films share similar social allusions such as reassignment of power and representation of different social groups in the flux of social change.

The importance of formalism in *Happy* also rests on Hitchcock's fantasy of probing for the "oooh" and "aaah" spots in the brain of the audience. Since Ah Gump does not mind copying, the images in his film are like a collage of many known elements. If the audience is familiar with any of these elements, their perception of these images has added dimensions. To appreciate singing and dancing in *Happy*, those who know *West Side Story* will see doomed love set in a backdrop of urban youth reclaiming territories. Those familiar with *Chicago* will think of the sarcasm on the legends the city of Chicago lives on. Those who have seen *Moulin Rouge* will recall love, death, and resurrection expressed in an atmosphere of high-society decadence. Those who watched *Memories of Matsuko* will understand how joy produces and sharpens pain in one's life. Those familiar with Bollywood films will have complex association with many Indian stories. All and any of these can be helpful added dimensions for an enriched understanding of the film *Happy*.

An important formal element in *Happy* is the metaphorical treatment of the pair of red dancing shoes that belong to the massage girl but are worshipped by Gao Xing. At a moment in *Happy*, this pair of shoes wins Gao Xing a kiss from the massage girl and leads them into a dance soon joined by many. The dance features the lyrics of "*Wei shen me ne?*" (Why?), which questions the low social status of rural migrants in the city. The dance sends the migrants' dreams flying into the sky—with the screen showcasing soaring toy planes made of folded paper. The allusion of the dancing shoes illustrates the in-between nature again. They may lead the audience to think of the Cinderella story and be optimistically sympathetic with the massage girl. The shoes, nonetheless, also refer to a similar use of dancing shoes in *Memories of Matsuko*, where shoes represent Matsuko's vain effort to win her father's love and her unrealistic wish to dance in "Alice's Wonderland," both of which are used to emphasize her misfortunes and disappointments in life. For the love story in *Happy*, this association adds some underdeveloped elements in the film. The red dancing shoes, for some audiences, may also recall the world of *Moulin Rouge*, where dancing celebrates romantic love triumphing over material wealth. In this pair of shoes, memories, myth, an existential testimony, and a legend all mingle and mix.

A major factor that inspired Ah Gump to be formalistic and to join the *egao* trend is the impact of *Crazy Stone*. It takes Ah Gump several years and a couple other *egao* films to let the formula of comedy plus elements inspired by Forrest Gump to succeed for him. In *Happy*, his lead characters, the country boy (Guo Tao) and the city boy (Huang Bo) are both lead actors from *Crazy Stone*. *Egao* allows *Happy* to merge into the popularity of *Forrest Gump*, that is, to the attention of ordinary folks. In China's general political culture, this style allows *Happy* to position itself on the margin of the cultural mainstream and to become part of the cultural hooliganism first initiated by the Beijing-based writer Wang Shuo. Just as Wang Shuo popularizes Beijing dialect through his works, many *egao* works and recent films in China draw linguistic strength from various local dialects, aimed at assuring a more quintessential connection with the grassroots. *Happy*, in this sense, can take credit for winning a popular love for Shannxi dialect by having fully explored its linguistic subtleties and musical capabilities. *Happy*'s use of the Xi'an-based band Heisa has greatly enlivened this particular version of the Chinese "Ode to Joy" in Shannxi dialect.

The need for commercial success motivates film director Ah Gump to better connect with his ever-diversifying, hybrid audience, which is sustained by the abundance of materials from an ill-regulated video market. Selling films here is not a far cry from selling other commodities in the globalized market; the mechanism of connecting buyers and commodities testifies to changes in world politics. One of the changes, as Benjamin Barber describes, is how "hard power yields to soft, while ideology is transmuted into a kind of videology that works through sound bites and film clips" (Barber 1996, 17). While videology reconnects the globe, correspondence occurs between street and virtual realities, rendering audiences into a more complex in-betweenness of fuzzier video moments. The borders in this wide visual whole are indeed becoming harder to draw but idealism, or Spinozian desire for happiness as a driving force for life, helps initiate traffic of video materials and produces cohesion points of needs for video traffic. The local politics, as shown in our discussion of *Happy*, still dictate particular retrievals of globalized formal elements.

4   CRAZY RACER: TO CONSTRUCT A NING HAO BRAND

Creating the sequel to a successful film is always a challenge since it risks being a disappointment in comparison. Three years after *Crazy Stone*, Ning Hao produced *Crazy Racer* (Fengkuang de saiche, 2009). Set in the seaside city Xiamen, *Crazy Racer* is interwoven with at least four groups of characters crisscrossing in three storylines. Line 1, to bury a father-like coach: Geng Hao, the protagonist, narrowly loses a gold medal in an international cycling race and is subsequently disqualified for using illegal performance-enhancing substances when he is duped into sponsoring an energy drink by crooked businessman Li Fala. After his coach (who lives with Geng as a father figure) dies of a heart attack, Geng becomes obsessed with seeking retribution from Li to pay for the coach's funeral. He works as a truck driver for seafood delivery. He and his freezer truck unwittingly cross the paths of criminals from other narrative lines. Line 2, to kill a wife: Li Fala wants his dictatorial wife killed and hires two migrant workers who claim to be professional killers. Soon he discovers that his hired killers want him dead, since they fail to kill the wife and are reemployed by her. When Li kills his wife on his own and obtains the payment she prepared for the killers, Geng arrives to claim his money. Li gives Geng the sum he just obtained but soon starts to frame Geng as his wife's killer. Line 3, to obtain a drug shipment: a group of Taiwan triad society members come to Xiamen to pick up a drug shipment from Chacai, a fake cyclist of the Thai delegation, who is accidentally frozen to death by Li's hired killers, using Geng's truck, and whose frozen body is then delivered to Geng. Geng is now wanted both by the police and by the triad society. He is constantly on the run; in one sequence, he steals a racer's uniform and bicycle to escape from a police hunt but ends up winning the gold medal for that race. What he and his coach once devoted their lives to obtain is now just a fleeting episode in his run from the bitter jokes life has in store for him.

Although *Crazy Racer* was another box office hit, many critics believed that it was not as artistically successful as *Crazy Stone*. Comparison indeed produced disappointment. In 2009, when several leading film scholars gathered at *Contemporary Film* journal to discuss this film with Ning Hao, however, they were not focusing on comparing the artistic merits of the two films. Instead, they were more concerned about building a Ning Hao brand (Fig. 4.6). The scholars wanted to explore (1) how Ning Hao himself needed to respond to the "2008 Ning Hao effects" in which a group of films repeated his style of multiple story lines, grassroots characters,

Fig. 4.6 *Crazy Racer.* To construct a Ning Hao brand

absurd stories concerning gangsters, and the use of black humor; (2) the possibility of "packaging" (da bao) these films to increase their commercial success and cultural impact; (3) the need to analyze the audience expectations contained in Ning Hao's commercial success; and (4) the opportunity of nourishing the Chinese audience's tendency to see a film because of its director alone—just like how audiences tend to anticipate Hong Kong director Stephen Chow's new films (Zheng Dongtian et al. 2009). These concerns helped broaden the scope in understanding *Crazy Racer* and reduced the intensity of disappointment. In line with the idea of a Ning Hao brand, another critic connects the two films by using French theorist Tiphane Samoyault's concept of intertextuality primarily from a commercial sense—how the first film becomes a "commercial resource" for the second one, how the second film needs to accept the challenge of specified audience expectations because of the first film, how websites need to be better used to enlarge the fan groups, and how "culture and economy need to collaborate" to assure the success of the two related cultural commodities (Zhang Yue 2009). Often, the initial film has already opened up the relationship between a film text and the texts of society and culture. The later films, by joining the social event of the initial film (the formulation of fan groups and the circulation of related dis- courses), is called upon more to continue a style—*Crazy Racer* needs to reward the "returned customer" with new twist and turns of Ning-Hao- style cuts and camera angles, multiple storylines filled with coincidences, stories that transpire as roller-coaster rides, entertaining dialogues in diver- sified dialects, and humor expressed in dead seriousness.

The concept of "Ning Hao brand films" shows Chinese scholars' emerging respect for the film market. In 2006, when *Crazy Stone* was enjoying the praise of many critics, the Beijing Film Academy professor Liu Yibin wrote an article to express his amazement; he believes that there is nothing particularly artistic or *avant-garde* about *Crazy Stone* except that it closely follows the genre recipe based on the commercial experi- ences of the Western film industry (Liu Yibin 2007). For him, Ning Hao is like his best student who studies the genre recipes well and Sinicizes them in his films' details. With this observation, Liu pleads for well-made commercial genre films in China, regrets that there are still discrimination against studying films as cultural commodities (that need to sell well). Liu also reflects on the post-Mao trajectory of the proposal of this same idea using a different term, "entertainment film" (yule pian), since "commer- cial films" may allude to money, the all-sinful money. Liu's idea here touches upon an underlying theme of the two rounds of "craziness films" that we are investigating—these films are box-office winners by either keeping a distance from or directly challenging contemporary art-house films. Ning Hao echoes Liu's idea in a later interview (Ning Hao and Wu Guanping 2009). He believes that 80 percent of all films rely on "telling the stories well" (guigui juju jiang gushi). "There is a rich store," he says, "of rules and norms for storytelling—what object or what sign will pro- duce what effects or will give what stimulus to the audience" (Ning Hao and Wu Guanping 2009, 72). In this sense, film directors for him are like engineers "doing technical work" according to the need of his audience. The other 20 percent of films, according to him, do not rely much on stories, such as documentary films or some *avant-garde* films. Ning Hao believes that the eighty/twenty ratio also accounts for that of the general needs of all audiences. Considering China's out-of-proportion emphasis on art-house films, Ning Hao deplores that in China 80 percent of work and resources are devoted to the needs of 20 percent of the total audience.

The multiple-story-line narrative that is true to both *Crazy Racer* and *Crazy Stone* is an essential feature of the Ning Hao brand. It is a playful feature that connects well with younger generations among the Chinese audience who have grown up playing electronic games and who are more attuned to fantasy rather than realistic portrayals of the world. Zhang Wei, in surveying the 2009 Chinese film market, observes a generational mismatch between film producers, born primarily in the 1950s and 1960s in the era of socialist realism, and the majority of Chinese filmgoers, born since the 1980s, who are wild about anything that is not real, as attested by the huge box office success in China of James Cameron's *Avatar* (Zhang Wei 2010). The multiple-story-line narrative, through its alienation effect very much like Brecht describes it for theater, may render a real-life story game-like. Relatedly, the subject of organized crime in these films, as a Chinese film critic observes, has also turned from the truthful portrayal of a social phenomenon to being used as more entertaining elements (Zheng Dongtian et al. 2009). The Chinese portrayal of triad society, Ning Hao assures us, "is all coming from films" (Ning Hao and Wu Guanping 2009, 74). In other words, it is the product of a cinephilia.

Crazy Stone executes multiple-story lines effectively since the central object of the film, that precious stone of jade, relates all the characters and narrative lines. Thus the stone functions well as what people in the film business call a MacGuffin, that is, as Hitchcock explains it, a plot device that motivates the characters and advances the story. In the film, the jade stone can change lives for over 200 factory employees, testify to the ego and manhood of the security chief Bao, increase the sexual and financial appeal of a dandy boy, empower an unethical real estate developer, secure the reputation of a professional Hong Kong thief, and mirror the stupidity of a group of conmen dreaming of the big time. As a typical central object in the genre of treasure-hunt stories, this MacGuffin ties together layers of confrontations of all involved. It testifies to Ning Hao's love for the techniques of storytelling. To reflect postmodern pastiche and trickery, this MacGuffin also gathers sarcastically many other genre styles, such as the longing and betrayal of a romantic film, the pettiness and vulgarity of a plebian farce, the suspense and pursuit of a detective film, and the contrast of ordinary people and triad society in a gangster film. In this sense, it is no wonder that Chinese scholars apply Mikhail Bakhtin's literary concepts of "heteroglossia" and "polyphony" to the interpretation of these two Ning Hao films—speech and complex cultural discourses mishmash in genres by means of heteroglossia (*egao* definitely has its ways of including other's words, speeches, or expressions), which renders works polyphonous (including multiple voices, styles, references, and assumptions).[14]

Furthermore, since this MacGuffin relays all the implications produced by the story, it can also easily become allegorical, seen for example as Sisyphus' stone as discussed by Albert Camus.

To continue the game-like spell of *Crazy Stone, Crazy Racer* becomes more ambitious but faces the challenge of putting together not only multiple narrative lines but also multiple stories. Midway in the production, Ning Hao realizes many potential shortcomings of this not-so-traditional way of storytelling, such as the film time needed to tell all the stories that may deprive the film of other elements and the constant shifting perspectives that may confuse audience. Still, he decides to confront these since his primary goal for doing this film is "a technical training of evolved film narration," and he has the Coen brothers' films to model after (Ning Hao and Wu Guanping 2009). If one looks for a MacGuffin in *Crazy Racer* that connects all the stories and characters, one may be led first to Geng's freezer truck; it advances the stories well but does not always motivate the characters. It also does not connect the two bicycle races, which in contrast, are crucial to the meaning of the film. For *Crazy Racer*, one has to go for a broader sense of MacGuffin to include film characters. Geng is not only the sole person in the film who connects all other characters and events, but he is also the person who holds answers to all the mysteries to film characters (including himself). Eventually, most of the mystery-driven characters in the film meet in the stadium not only to find answers but also to witness the absurdity of Geng winning a gold medal with a mistaken identity, which suggests the nature of his unwitting knowledge.

Ning Hao's storytelling skills in *Crazy Racer* can be further appreciated by referring to Robert McKee's popular book *Story: Substance, Structure, Style, and the Principles of Screenwriting* (Yang Di 2010). Published in China in 2001, the book is used by both the Beijing Film Academy and China's Central Academy of Drama. Since 2011, McKee has visited China several times, giving warmly received screenwriting seminars. McKee's popularity confirms many ideas by Liu and Ning that we have just discussed. Here the reference is to the art of "setups," which as McKee explains, "must be planted in such a way that when the audience first sees them, they have one meaning, but with a rush of insight, they take on a second, more important meaning. It's possible that a single setup may have meanings hidden to a third or fourth level" (McKee 1998, 240). When several stories are unfolded in a crisscross way, setup serves not only one story but is more likely to be picked up in other stories to both solve an old riddle and give rise to new suspense. This netting use of setups helps to both engage audiences and clarify stories. "To set up," McKee explains, "means to layer in knowledge; to pay off means to close the gap by delivering that knowledge to the audience" (McKee 1998, 238). Reviewers are generally amazed by the great number of cuts that Ning Hao has to use in *Crazy Racer* to cram the film with all the necessary elements and layers of knowledge to tell several stories. This abundance of setups and payoffs is never dull. Viewers responses agree: the film is like "a constantly delayed showing of answers to a series of riddles"; it produces "a unique (in the sense of strangeness) sort of happiness"; its "high density use of cuts produces a rhythmic joy as that of a Chinese tongue twister";[15] it "induces collective, brainy whirlwinds among the audience"; and it is a "game-like carnival" (Wang Chao 2009; Yang Di 2010).

To turn from using an object to using a character as the MacGuffin, *Crazy Racer* is believed to be darker and more absurd in its outlook to contemporary Chinese life. The jade stone in *Crazy Stone* may induce all sorts of craziness, but it also functions as a value anchor to contrast the ethical craziness for hundreds of potentially unemployed workers with the craziness for unethical gains, or even to contrast the efforts to regain manhood for the security chief, the main con man, and the dandy boy. Geng in *Crazy Racer* does not have this function for value differentiation but rather for increasing the sense of absurdity. As a Chinese reviewer observes, if it is not for Geng's involvement, such events as an athlete dreaming of a gold medal, an unethical merchant promoting questionable products, sudden wealth alienating husband and wife, triad society dealing in illegal drugs, and small-time cops eager to solve a big-time case may all appear "normal." What is so abnormal is that Geng connects them all, bringing doom on all involved and upon himself because of these connections (Zhou Yang 2009). When he sustains all the doom and pain of all the events, Geng personifies the film's statement that "the world is absurd and human life is painful" (Zhou Yang 2009).

The contrast of the two MacGuffins also accounts for some of the disappointment over *Crazy Racer*, primarily because of the film's value ambiguity. Li Yunlei comments on the conceitedness of *Crazy Racer* in storytelling and in the ability to connect multiple stories. He nonetheless believes the film's showcasing of stories is just the other side of the same coin of contemporary Chinese blockbuster films' inability to come up with forceful stories (Li Yunlei 2009). Both the skillful navigation among stories and the lack of convincing stories, to him, derive from China's crisis of value confusion and artists' inability to say anything insightful other than passively reflecting on the fragmented status of Chinese values. He believes that Ning Hao, by copying Guy Ritchie and Quentin Tarantino, has produced a work of black humor but one that lacks the philosophical pain in its use of pastiche and in showcasing fragmentation—its darkness is a far cry from the postmodern nihilism of the West. Wang Wenbin accuses *Crazy Racer* of being degraded from *Crazy Stone*'s realism to a pure vehicle for entertainment (Wang Wenbin 2009). He appreciates *Crazy Stone*'s *mise en scène*, believing it has all the virtue if one examines it according to film theorist Siegfried Kracauer's "street aesthetics." In contrast, he sees *Crazy Racer*'s *mise en scène* as artificial, a symptom of the nature of the whole film.

5   *Crazy Foolish Thieves*: Connections with Hong Kong

Knowing that the seed money for *Crazy Stone* is from Hong Kong and the film's central *egao* thrust can be traced to the influence of Hong Kong film director Stephen Chow, it is intriguing to use *Crazy Foolish Thieves* (Fengkuang de chunzei, 2012), a crime comedy inspired by *Crazy Stone* but primarily in reference of Hong Kong crime films, as an indicator of the cultural traffic between the mainland and Hong Kong concerning the impact of neo-noir (Fig. 4.7). Among varied channels of the genre's impact, this channel opened up by *egao* shows heavier traffic and more popular following. In contrast, a less noticed channel is that through culturally high-brow, art-house films. Take for example Hong Kong director Anne Hui. Her first feature film, *Crazy Secret* (Feng jie, 1980), a Hitchcock-like suspense drama about a real-life double murder, is often considered as a pioneering work among the early noir films in Asian. In 2006, she appears to be saluting *Crazy Stone*'s claim to postmodernism by showcasing her tragi-comic, neo-noir-ish *The Postmodern Life of My Aunt* (Yima de hou xiandai shenghuo). The attention she captured, however, was more of the reviewers of the international art-film circuit and less of a domestic audience in China. As a result, it did not establish its footing in the *Crazy Stone* discourse.

Obviously captured by the *egao* inspiration of *Crazy Stone*, *Crazy Foolish Thieves*—directed by Li Kai and showcasing Hong Kong gangster film stars Francis Ng and Suet Lam—wavered between two marketing strategies: to emphasize its Hong Kong reference or to feature its *Crazy Stone*

Fig. 4.7 *Crazy Foolish Thieves.* Hong Kong connections

connection. The film was initially named *Thief Affairs* (Dao zhong dao) to refer to the popular Hong Kong film *Infernal Affairs* (Wujian dao, 2002) but finally settled with *Crazy Foolish Thieves* to connect with Ning Hao's *Crazy Stone* and *Crazy Racer*. After six years, Ning's popularity was still growing.

Crazy Foolish Thieves (*Thieves* hereafter) tells the story of a heist gone bad. To evade debt, Hong Kong mobster Lok (Francis Ng) takes refuge in mainland China at the home of friend Xiaobao, a huge fan of Hong Kong gangster movies who dreams of becoming a tough guy. In order to pay back his debt, Lok plans to rob the residence of wealthy businessman Wang Shixiong and ropes in Xiaobao to assist him. During the theft, they run into Blue (Suet Lam), known as "No.1 Killer of Southeast Asia," hired to murder Wang. It appears that Blue, a clown who is also deep in debt, has been hired by both the son (Jack) and the daughter (Shiyi) of Wang in their struggle for inheritance. Chaotically, neither the robbers nor the murderer succeed in Wang's apartment, and Wang ends up in a coma. Wang's attorney reveals a condition of Wang's will that if the son and daughter cannot inherit together, the family wealth goes to charity. In the meantime, another incident leads Shiyi to lose her memory so that she forgets her identity and remains a young woman who relies solely on her "batman" Lok, who rescues her from drowning. Jack, now knowing the condition of the will, starts a desperate search first for his missing sister and then for someone who can pass for her. Lok has fallen in love with Shiyi while caring for her and soon finds that he has to resist the temptation of offering her to Jack as someone who can pass as the daughter for the reward. Shiyi regains her memory at a crucial moment only to discover that her father is already broke and all the conflict over inheritance becomes meaningless.

With the presence of Francis Ng and Suet Lam, the twin-treasures of Hong Kong gangster films in portraying viciousness (*ye*) and frivolity (*pi*), *Thieves* wants its audience to be reminded of their roles in many previous films. As an *egao* film relying on sarcastic parodies to entertain its audience, *Thieves* conjures a range of Hong Kong films and is thus caught in the middle of the cultural traffic between mainland China and Hong Kong. Following these connections may allow us to see how the film is affected by multiple cultural orientations. Taking a step back, we want to see how the film, like a spider, hangs on a cultural web.

The range of these Hong Kong films begins with Andrew Lau's *Young and Dangerous* (Guhuozai zhi ren zai jianghu, 1996); *Thieves* imitates *Young and Dangerous* by inserting caricature paintings to introduce and comment on its characters. On the surface, the connection appears to be a retrieval of the celebration of the youthful energy shown in that film, which has an interesting resemblance to the origins of mainland Fifth Generation filmmaking and the directors' interest in showcasing anti-heroes and celebrating the energy of life. The on-the-site style of *Young and Dangerous* also resembles the contemporary Sixth Generation directors' use of gritty realism. *Young and Dangerous* vividly depicts a group of young members of Hong Kong triad society, about their growth, adventures, loyalty, and love. Although there have been accusations that the film has glorified the gangsters, it remains immensely popular not only in Hong Kong but also among the mainland's young audience. The adventures of these youthful characters have become legendary. If one dislikes the fact that Lam is missing and Ng plays an anti-youth villain in *Young and Dangerous*, filmic associations also lead to *The Mission* (Qianghuo, 1999), which uses *Young and Dangerous'* theme music and caricature paintings in the credit sequence and which features both Ng and Lam as young gangsters who develop an unusual friendship in fulfilling a gang mission. Ng and Lam are called upon to remind the Chinese audience of a Hong Kong cult.

Thieves' connection with *Young and Dangerous* is thus more than that of films; it is a moment of Chinese youth culture, in the black carnival playfulness, retrieving an attractive moment of Hong Kong's film culture. *Young and Dangerous* is the beginning of a series of about a dozen young gangster films (*guhuo zai* in Hong Kong dialect) produced in a half dozen of Hong Kong's *fin de siècle* years. This eruption of films had its popular followers; the cartoon journal from which *Young and Dangerous* obtains its title had already boasted staggering sale records of 20,000 to 30,000 copies for its monthly issues. This popular display of feelings through cinema consists of primarily quickly produced films that cater fans, but it also incorporates *avant-garde* artistic explorations. Ka-fai Wai's 1997 film *Too Many Ways to Be Number One* (Yige zitou de dan sheng) is not only a typical example of Hong Kong neo-noir elaborating a sense of doom but also an artistic gem featuring unique camera angles and movements related to the chaotic feelings of the characters, as well as parallel, *Blind Chance* kind of story lines showing different (but equally doomed) life options for the characters. Another example that is particularly important to our discussion—since Francis Ng played the leading role and established his fame by winning Hong Kong Film Reviewer Society's "Best Actor Award"—is *Once Upon a Time in Triad Society* (Wangjiao zha FIT ren, 1996). Resembling the narrative structure of showing parallel stories of a same person's life in *Too Many Ways to Be Number One*, this film, in first person narrative, also presents parallel, contradicting stories of the rise and fall of a triad society leader.

It appears as though these two films were having a dialogue with *Young and Dangerous*, which reiterates a utopian ideology of Hong Kong grassroots society as expressed in gangster films of the 1950s and 1960s. This utopian ideology, as Xu Le phrases it, is expressed as "I help others; others help me (*wo wei ren ren, ren ren wei wo*)":

> A plebeian society defines inter-person relationship as that of mutual assistance and love … It is an extension of Confucian dictum, "to honor old people as we do our own aged parents, and care for other's children as one's own" … [This ideology] suits the Chinese living in a British colony. (Xu Le 2015, 52)

This ideology has long helped ordinary people in Hong Kong (the grassroots) to maintain their Chinese identity in a colonial society. The youthful gangsters in *Young and Dangerous* confirm the myth that good guys in the triad society may keep the bad guys under control (*xie hei bu sheng zheng hei*). If this reiteration by *Young and Dangerous* reflects what Xu Le calls "Hong Kong people's self-anaesthetization" (Xu Le 2006, 7) while they confront the uncertainty of the island's 1997 return to China, the other two films' noir element, either seriously doomed or mischievously sarcastic, becomes the awakening undertones of that historical display of feelings. Facing the same crisis caused by political uncertainty (how the new rulers compare with the British), these films chose not to believe in the fairy tales of brotherhood but focused more on depicting society as a jungle and conveying the sense of doom and decline of the Confucian gangster ideology.

Thieves is drawn to this moment in Hong Kong film culture owing to its own concern for the masses, which is a major branch of the *Crazy Stone* discourse, and its connection with contemporary Chinese plebeian distrust of government and official ideology. As an *egao* film, *Thieves* is caught between two moments of political uncertainty. It focuses on the yearning for heroes, but it also inherits the anti-romantic undercurrents of the Hong Kong historical moment. It starts by showing cartoon frames of the lead (Frances Ng) as powerful (muscular) Batman who may rescue the Chinese youth grown up watching Hong Kong films but, throughout the film, by means of *egao* sarcasm, undermines this expectation.

Thieves' appeal to the masses and effort to redefine success can be vindicated by Francis Ng and Suet Lam showing up in another film produced in the mainland in the same year, *Good-for-nothing Heroes* (Qing jiao wo yingxiong, 2012). In this comic film, Ng and Lam get into another heritage competition. Lam and his friend Pang are trash kings of an old neighborhood; by discovering an important will, Lam aids Pang in becoming one of the successors of a five-star hotel. While the writer of the will is lying in a coma (first real and then feigned), Pang and the hotel owner's adopted son, played by Ng, start a business war against each other. Ng appears to have gained an upper hand since he is a shrewd person who understands hotel business; Pang, in contrast, cannot forget his friends from the old neighborhood including a blind girl he loves. Pang wants his business to help rebuild that neighborhood; Pang's concern for the grassroots (observed secretly by the hotel owner) has proven him a worthy successor. Juxtaposing these two films allows us to see that Hong Kong actors were tackling particular Chinese mainland issues such as people's adjustment to the market-oriented society. Both films draw attention to the corrupting power of money and to the contrast of it with the warmth of human feelings (love, friendship, and community).

Helping the mainland Chinese, Hong Kong filmmakers were also help-ing themselves. Following the political uncertainty of 1997, Hong Kong was besieged by the devastating financial crisis in Asia and its film industry was on the point of bankruptcy. In the end of 2003, mainland and Hong Kong issued "Closer Economic Partnership Arrangement" (CEPA), which was translated in Hong Kong film industry as "bei shang jiu shi" (to ven-ture into the mainland for the market rescue). With this large-scale historic move, Hong Kong film reviewers started to refer to Hong Kong films since 2004 as "post-Hong Kong films," "neo pier films," "pan Chinese films," or "Hong-Kong-produced cooperation films." Hong Kong film-makers had to investigate the taste buds of the mainland audience and to adjust the flavor of their films. They also had to consider the requirements of the mainland government's censorship. The result, as observed by Chinese film scholars, was the loss of "Hong Kong flavor shown in exag-geration (*guohuo*) and craziness (*diankuang*)" (Xu and Hao 2011, 2). Stephen Chow's films since 2004, for example, have lost much of the features that captured Chinese mainland youth in a whirlwind years back.

The two Ng-and-Lam films of 2012, in this perspective, are both caught between the challenge of keeping or losing Hong Kong flavor. In contrast, since *Please Call Me Hero* is not caught up in the ripple effects of *Crazy Stone*, on the one hand, it has succeeded in ridding itself of Hong Kong vulgarity. *Thieves*, on the other hand, retained crucial crew members and actors from the *Crazy Stone* team and intended to let the Hong Kong stars further the ripple effects of *egao*. In *Thieves*, *egao* craziness and Hong-Kong-flavor craziness combined to resonate and to keep the sublimation (as an antidote for Hong Kong flavor) from taking over. In *Thieves*, many elements—such as the landlady's crush on Lok and their simulated sex act or the training of Xiao Bao by asking him to harass a woman—are likely to be the type of scenes that the other films would delete in an effort to avoid Hong Kong vulgarity.

The kinship of *egao* craziness and Hong-Kong-flavor craziness suggest similar social reasons for the common folks to vent unhappiness. Stephen Chow's earlier *wunitou* comedies (like films produced by Michael Hui in the 1970s and the 1980s) won a popular following on the basis of their Hong Kong style. The word craziness, it is interesting to note, also showed up in the titles of comedies then, such as *Crazy Crooks* (Fengkuang da laoqian, 1980) and *Crazy Games* (Fengkuang youxi, 1985). Chinese scholars define Hong Kong comedies as "plebeian comedies" and "farces that are suitable for plebeian carnival" (Xu and Hao 2011, 3). They relate this type of comedy to "Hong Kong's all-around economic take off (as that of a plane)" and while the masses contributed to the economy, they also faced dislocation and anger because of it (Xu and Hao 2011, 3). Chow's comedies, according to them, brought a sense of "confusion" and "exile" because of the new crisis caused by Hong Kong's return to China (Xu and Hao 2011, 3). Mainland China's economic take off, with the Tian'anmen Square massacre as an indication, requires an enforced cynicism of "shut up and get rich." Ordinary folks' dislocation and frustration because of this boom is bound to have a lot of political anxiety involved. It is not accidental that Chow's comedies could induce school campus carnivals in mainland China and, in many ways, this carnival paved the way for the outburst of the *Crazy Stone* carnival of 2006.

Among the Hong Kong films that *Thieves* builds *egao* connections with are the three *Infernal Affairs* films that enjoyed international fame and even prompted Martin Scorsese's American adaptation, *The Departed* (2006). Audiences laugh when Ng jeers at his own acting in those films, brags that *Infernal Affairs* is based on his real life, and describes his current role in *Thieves* a batman disguised as an ordinary person living in a poor neighborhood ("a spy with double identity"). The initial *Infernal Affairs* is also directed by *Young and Dangerous*' Andrew Lau. Knowing Lau's role in Ringo Lam's *City on Fire* (1987) and Wong Kar-wai's *Chungking Express* (1994), one can be sure that he brought with him elements of Hong Kong neo-noir. The success of the film relies less on violence and action and more on the internal turmoil of the spies and their confusion about identities, with the grim depiction of a drug war as the backdrop. Allegorically, just as the anxiety over the expiration dates of processed food in *Chungking Express*, the anxiety with personal identities of the spies has been read as the lingering expression of crisis caused by Hong Kong's return to China. The sense of confusion lends a dark feeling to the film. The unsettling ending of the film also goes well with a noir film: it is the cop spy who dies and the gangster spy who successfully cuts ties with triad society, decides to hide his tainted past, and is ready to start a new episode of life as if nothing had ever happened. *Thieves*, in *egao* parody, renders a similar ending to denounce the rule of money. In the film, Batman, along with Spiderman and Superman, is an indication not of power but the cleverness of scheming to make money or foolishness of being enslaved by money. All the major players of the inheritance war wear Batman or Spiderman costumes at various moments. To end the film, Lok, as the Batman spy (a Batman disguised as an ordinary person), finally realizes the shame of being a Batman. He uses the three-year jail term to break away from his past and starts a new life as a changed, "fertile" person (a joke that his transformation will give birth to many who choose to do just the same as him).

Comparing *Young and Dangerous* with *Infernal Affairs*, one is impressed by the changes in their film stories and *mise en scènes*: from mean streets to high-rise buildings, from valor in fighting to wisdom of scheming, from winning with muscles to winning by information, and from low tech to high tech. These changes obviously opened doors for later hit Hong Kong films such as "the three wars": *The Viral Factor* (Ni zhan, 2011), *Cold War* (Han zhan, 2012), and *Drug War* (Du zhan, 2013). With this film world update, there is also a noticeable change in the dominant ideology of these films. With *Cold War* as the most typical example, the ideology shifts from Confucian/gangster culture described before to the Western ideology of institutional checks and balances, regulations, and law. Just as Confucian/gangster ideology allowed the people of Hong Kong a space for identity in a colonial society, this new ideology lends Hong Kong filmmakers new room for cultural critique while collaborating with a non-elected totalitarian government.[16]

Thieves, as a low-budget film, did not have much room for this updating. All the changes, however, embed seeds in the career of *Thieves'* director Li Kai. What Li Kai brings to *Thieves* are his interests in Chinese youth literature (such as Anni Babei's works), his film art training as Chen Kaige's assistant, and his enthusiasm for *egao*, having worked as the associate director of *Crazy Stone*. *Thieves* strengthened Li Kai's Hong Kong connection. In 2014, he directed *War on a String* (Xuan zhan) that, though not a joint-produced film between Hong Kong and the mainland, obviously intended to join the array of "the three war" hit films.[17] The film was advertised as a noir suspense and a cop-and-gangster film. What is most interesting about *War on a String* is its male lead, an established attorney who decides to take justice into his own hands and who uses his wits to have money stolen from gangsters used not only to save his own sick daughter, but also for philanthropy. The new ideology concerning law in this type of film becomes its central subject.

Notes

1. Here is how the platform uses Liu Zhenyun, an invited-speaker, to illustrate its theme of "storytelling and story selling": "Liu's cold humor, his broad familiarity with the many facets of urban society, and his modern sensibilities have made him a favorite among Chinese readers. On a list published in November 2012, titled '2012 Writers Ranking—Rich and Influential,' Liu Zhenyun ranked 19th, with an income of 2.8 Million RMB in royalties" (http://www.storydrivechina.com/en2013/Speakers/speaker.php?id=3, accessed Jan. 29, 2016).

2. Graduating from China's Central Academy of Drama, Ma Liwen had a fairly successful start of her directing career. Her directorial debut, *Gone Is the One Who Held Me Dearest in the World* (2002), won her five awards China and abroad. In 2005, she directed *You and Me*, which uses her own script and showcases an unusual friendship between a twenty-something tenant and a ninety-something landlady in a Beijing courtyard. It won her a Golden Rooster award for Best Director in the same year.

3. This sarcasm is actually not incidental. Ma is fairly particular about her actor selection. For this film, she selects seven known film producers, scriptwriters, cinematographers, and directors to convey certain character traits and sarcasm that professional actors cannot always express.

4. The film's title credits show Feng Chao as the scriptwriter and director. Feng Chao also showed up accordingly in the film's marketing process. In 2009, however, after two years' deliberation, a court in Beijing ruled that Feng Chao be penalized for usurping the names of Bai Qiulin, who actually directed the film, and Feng Yun, who actually wrote the script. It appears that Bai Qiulin signed a contract to direct the film but not to do the post-production work, which was obviously masterminded by Feng Chao who had a close connection with the company that issued this film. Feng Chao's father was among the executives of the company.

5. The impact of *Crazy Stone* on these two titles is unmistakable. *The Second Best* claims to be the same kind of film as *Crazy Stone* and *My Own Swordsman* in advertising. Wang Yuelun, the director of *Almost Perfect*, starts an interview with Wu Guanping by talking about how he analyzes the success formula of *Crazy Stone* to work out his own style of the film. See Wu Guanping (2010, 89).

6. Shang Jing, the director and co-scriptwriter of *My Own Swordsman*, was invited by Zhang Yimou to become one of the scriptwriters of *A Simple Noodle Story*. Yan Ni, who played the innkeeper in *My Own Swordsman*, also became an innkeeper in Zhang's film.

7. *China Can Say No: Political and Emotional Choices in the Post-Cold-War Era* (Zhongguo keyi shuo bu: lengzhan hou shidai de zhengzhi yu qinggan jueze), published in 1996, marks a surge of nationalism in China. The

book, authored by several writers, is modeled after *Japan Can Say No*, a political essay published in Japan in 1989 advocating Japan's taking a more independent stance on business issues and foreign affairs.

8. In his book, *The Coen Brothers: Interview*, William Rodney Allen comments on how the Coen brothers use cinematic genres "to pay homage and simultaneously to introduce an element of mockery." Also see Renzi (2012).

9. This overall change does not keep nationalism from playing crucial roles in international politics nor America from becoming a frequent target of severe criticism backed up by popular feelings. See for example Song Xiaojun et al. (2009). The change, however, stops America from being a generalized enemy based primarily on ideological reasons, and it returns America to a real political power that needs analysis and understanding.

10. Ah Gump's real name is Liu Xiaoguang. He grew up in Xi'an and graduated from Xi'an University of Electronic Technology. *Happy* is set in his home city.

11. *West Side Story* is well-known and popular in China. It is in the "100 Titles of Required Viewing" list for the students of Beijing Film Academy. Before Ah Gump became a film director, he had worked for a company cataloging its collection of foreign film DVDs, which, in addition to his personal interest, gave him a fairly wide exposure to foreign films.

12. The band *Heisa* (Black Head) started to upload its lyrics online in 2003, and band members claim that they want to rejuvenate Shannxi dialect once used by the First Emperor of China. Their lyrics combine Shannxi local opera singing (*qin qiang*) with hip-hop, blues, jazz, and many other metal elements. Many praised *Heisa* for allowing them to rediscover the beauty of Shannxi dialect.

13. Formalism is Ah Gump's reference to his interest in stylistic enrichment. It is a rather innocent term and should not be confused with the same term that refers to a literary movement.

14. Mikhail Bakhtin's concept of "carnival" is widely referred to in the Chinese discourse about Ning Hao's crazy-titled films. For the reference of his concept of "polyphony," see Guo Cen (2009). Bakhtin's impact in Chinese academia is fairly substantial. In addition to separate titles of translation, his complete works were translated by Qian Zhongwen and published in seven volumes in 1998.

15. The effect of a Chinese tongue twister here, for those who are not familiar with it, can be imagined by thinking of rapping in hip-hop music.

16. Chinese scholar Xu Le discusses this ideological change in Hong Kong films but argues that the new ideology is the result of Hong Kong filmmakers yielding to the requirement of the Chinese central government. See Xu Le (2015).

17. "The three war hit films" refer to a surge in mainland-Hong Kong co-produced crime thrillers in 2012 and 2013. They include *Cold War* (Han zhan, 2012), *Adverse War/Viral Factor* (Ni zhang, 2012), and *Drug War* (Du zhan, 2013). The impact to these films is Johnny To's classic in this genre, *Hidden War/Running Out of Time* (An zhan, 1999).

REFERENCES

CHINESE LANGUAGE SOURCES

Anon. 2010. Daoyan Ah Gan de ziliao (Data About Director Ah Gump), posted February 26, 2010. http://zhidao.baidu.com/question/139379217.html. Accessed 10 May 2012.

Chen Linxia. 2010. *Sanqiang paian jingji* yu san ge beilun (*A Simple Noodle Story* and Three Paradoxes). *Yishu guangjiao* (Art Panorama) 2: 46–50.

Chen Mo. 2010. Wo kan 'sanqiang pai'an jingqi' (My View on *A Simple Noodle Story*). *Dangdai dianying* (Contemporary Cinema) 2: 34–36.

Guo Cen. 2009. Lun 'fengkuang de saiche' xushi fengge (On the Narrative Style of *Crazy Racer*). *Dianying wenxue* (Film Literature) 19: 70–71.

Hu Puzhong. 2008. *Wo jiao liu yuejin*: shangye hua de jieji biaoda (*Lost and Found*: Commercialized Social Class Representation). *Dianying yishu* (Film Arts) 3: 55–57.

Lao Yang. 2009. Duihua daoyan A Gan (A Dialogue with Director Ah Gump), posted February 18, 2009. http://i.mtime.com/646748/blog/1692122/. Accessed 10 May 2012.

Li Yang. 2008. Youxi: liudong de xiandaixing (Game: Modernity in Fluidity). *Yishu pinglun* (Art Review) 3: 54–56.

Li Yunlei. 2009. Women weishenme er jiang gushi: cong *fengkuang de saiche* shuoqi (Why Do We Tell Stories: With *Crazy Racer* as a Point of Departure for Discussion). *Dianying yishu* (Film Arts) 2: 18–20.

Liu Yibin. 2007. Mo zhe 'fengkuang de shitou' guohe (Cross the River by the Foothold Guidance of "Crazy Stones"). *Dianying yishu* (Film Arts) 3: 76–78.

Liu Zhongze. 2013. Wangluo minzu zhuyi gainian bianxi (An Analysis of the Concept of Net Nationalism). *Beijing qingnian zhengzhi xueyuan xuebao* (Journal of Beijing Academy of Political Science) 1: 37–41.

Luo Luo. 2006. *Wulin waizhuan*: xinue wuxia er bu dianfu xiayi (*My Own Swordsman*: Teasing but not Undermining Martial Arts). *Nanqiang beidiao* (Accents North and South) 4: 11–12.

Ma Liwen, and Wu Quanping. 2008. Ta jiao Liu Yuejing: Ma Liwen fangtan (About Film *Lost and Found*: An Interview of Ma Liwen). *Dianying yishu* (Film Arts) 2: 76–79.

Ning Hao, and Wu Quanping. 2009. Jiang gushi shi yimen jishu huo—Ning Hao fangtan (Film Stories Are Told by Techniques—An Interview with Ning Hao). *Dianying yishu* (Film Arts) 2: 72–77.

Song Xiaojun, et al. 2009. *Zhongguo bugaoxing* (Unhappy China: The Great Time, Grand Vision and Our Challenges). Nanjing: Jiangsu renmin chubanshe.

Wang Chao. 2009. Dianying shoufa de bentuhua: *fengkuang de shitou* yu gai liqi de ying pian de bijiao fenxi (Local Application of Film Skills: A Comparison of *Crazy Stone* and Guy Richy Films). *Tianying pingjie* (Movie Review) 1: 51–52.

Wang Guojie. 2009. Xifang: chaoyue egao de pingminhua yishu (Parody: A Plebian Art That Transcends *Egao*). *Dianying wenxue* (Film Literature) 5: 14–15.

Wang Wenbin. 2009. Fengkuang yijiu, zhenshi bu zai: dui dianying fengkuang saiche de pipanxing kaocha (Madness Continues, Reality No More: A Critical Investigation of *Crazy Racing Car*). *Lilun yu chuangzuo* (Criticism and Creation) 128 (3): 102–104.

Wu Guanping. 2010. Wanluo wenhua yu kuaican dianying: Wang Yuelun fantan (Web Culture and Fast-Food Film: An Interview of Wang Yuelun). *Dianying yishu* (Film Arts) 2: 89–94.

Xu Gang, and Hao Chaoshuai. 2011. 'Diankuang' de zhenghou yu 'gangwei' de zong ji (Symptoms of Craziness and Traces of Hong Kong Flavor). *Beijing dianying xueyuan xuebao* (Journal of Beijing Film Academy) 3: 2–6.

Xu Le. 2006. Heibai senlin: xiang gang hei shehui pian de shehui wenhua zhenghou dujie (*Color of the Truth*: A Reading of Social and Cultural Symptoms of Hong Kong's Black Society Films). *Dianying yishu* (Film Arts) 4: 5–10.

———. 2015. Xianggang yingfeipian de xiandaixing sibian ji wenhua bianzou (Modernity Thinking and Changing Cultural Melodies in Hong Kong Gangster and Cop Films). *Dianying yishu* (Film Arts) 4: 51–55.

Yang Di. 2010 'Ye dian' yu 'fengkuang de saiche' zhi fubi pushe bijiao (A Comparative Study of the Use of FB in *One Night in Supermarket* and *Crazy Racer*). *Dianying pingjie* (Movie Review) 1: 38–39.

Zhang Wei. 2010. 2009 dianying shichang chongdu: 80 hou yu zhongguo dianying meixue (Re-examining 2009 Film Market: Post-80 Generation and Chinese Film Aesthetics). *Beijing dianying xueyuan xuebao* (Journal of Beijing Film Academy) 1: 29–30.

Zhang Yiwu. 2002. 'Kandie de yi dai' zai jueqi (The Rise of the "Disc-Watching Generation"). *Dangdai dianying* (Contemporary Cinema) 5: 20–21.

———. 2010. 'Sanqiang pai'an jingqi': cong xiju zhong chongxin xunzhao kenengxing (*A Simple Noodle Story*: Rediscovering Possibilities in a Comedy). *Dangdai dianying* (Contemporary Cinema) 2: 27–31.

Zhang Yue. 2009. Cong *fengkuang de saiche* kan guochan dianyng de huwen shengchan (*Crazy Racer* and Intertextual Production Among Chinese Films). *Dianying pingjie* (Movie Review) 6: 33 and 35.

Zheng Dongtian, et al. 2006. Xinzuo pingyi: *fengkuang de shitou* (Discussion of New Movies: On *Crazy Stone*). *Dangdai dianying* (Contemporary Cinema) 5: 15–20.

———. 2009. Xinzuo pingyi: *fengkuang de saiche* (Discussion of New Movies: On *Crazy Racer*). *Dangdai dianying* (Contemporary Cinema) 3: 37–44.

Zhou Quanxin. 2008. Bosha, zhuizhuo, xiyan: jiti de xixi yu kuanghuan (Killing, Chasing, Teasing: Mass Games and Carnivals). *Dianying wenxue* (Movie Literature) 23: 21–22.

Zhou Yang. 2009. Ning Hao 'fengkuang dianying' de cunzaizhuyi (Existentialism of Ning Hao's Crazy Films). *Shannxi shifan daxue xuebao* (Journal of Shaanxi Normal University—Philosophy and Social Sciences Edition) 38: 380–382.

ENGLISH LANGUAGE SOURCES

AP. 2010. Sick of All the On-screen Vomiting? posted March 1, 2010. http://www.theage.com.au/news/entertainment/film/articles/2010/03/01/1267291837148.html. Accessed 15 June 2012.

Bakhtin, M.M. 1984. *Problems of Dostoevsky's Poetics*. Ed. and Trans. Caryl Emerson. Minneapolis/London: University of Minnesota Press.

Barber, Benjamin R. 1996. *Jihad vs. McWorld: How Globalism and Tribalism Are Reshaping the World*. New York: Ballantine Books.

Billson, Anne. 2010. Vomit: The Recurring Movie Motif, posted May 6, 2010. http://www.guardian.co.uk/film/2010/may/06/vomit-movie-motif-taboo-billson. Accessed 15 June 2012.

Evans, Jonathan. 2014. Zhang Yimou's *Blood Simple*: Cannibalism, Remaking and Translation in World Cinema. *Journal of Adaptation in Film & Performance* 7 (3): 283–297.

Hassan, Ihab. 1986. Pluralism in Postmodern Perspective. *Critical Inquiry* 12 (3): 503–520.

Kuoshu, Harry. 2002. *Celluloid China: Cinematic Encounters with Culture and Society*. Carbondale/Edwardsville: Southern Illinois University Press.

Lee, Min. 2006. 2 Chinese Boys Lip-Sync Their Way to Web Stardom. Posted October 4, 2006. http://www.seattletimes.com/entertainment/2-chinese-boys-lip-sync-their-way-to-web-stardom/. Accessed 2 July 2016.

McKee, Robert. 1998. *Story: Substance, Structure, Style, and the Principles of Screenwriting*. New York: Methuen.

Morrow, Lance. 1992. Folklore in a Box. *Time*, September 21, 50.

Renzi, Thomas C. 2012. *Screwball Comedy and Film Noir: Unexpected Connections*. Jefferson: McFarland.

Spoto, Donald. 1984. *The Dark Side of Genius: The Life of Alfred Hitchcock*. New York: Ballantine Books.

Wang, Jennifer Hyland. 2000. A Struggle of Contending Stories: Race, Gender, and Political Memory in *Forrest Gump*. *Cinema Journal*, 39 (3): 92–115.

CHAPTER 5

Dual Retrieval of Cinematic Craziness: A Coda

Abstract This chapter uses two cinematic retrievals of craziness, one by Huang Bo in 2018 with his mini film *Crazy Twins* and the other by Ning Hao in 2019 with his film *Crazy Alien*, to both indicate the twelve-plus-year duration of this episode of cinematic craziness and use the discussion of the two films to summarize some common artistic features of the films produced in this episode. The first retrieval allows one to understand the character type created by Huang in the episode and the retrieval illustrates how an established actor feels the need to be crazy to remove the doldrums in his career. To be crazy is to rejuvenate. The second retrieval leads one to see how Ning Hao works on his story and script, how he retains his earlier "low-budget" styles of craziness in this expensive film, how he emphasizes his film being "postmodern," and how the monkey image becomes important in his filmmaking.

Keywords Huang Bo • Ning Hao • Ning Hao brand • Monkey King • Dirty monkey • Hollywood • Soy-sauce-jar culture • *Egao* parody • Postmodernism

In the 2018 Chinese New Year season, Huang Bo, who jump-started his acting career with *Crazy Stone*, issued a Kentucky Fried Chicken-sponsored mini film (just 10.5 minutes long) entitled *Crazy Twins* (Fengkuang de

© The Author(s), under exclusive license to Springer Nature Switzerland AG 2021
H. H. Kuoshu, *Craziness and Carnival in Neo-Noir Chinese Cinema*, Chinese Literature and Culture in the World, https://doi.org/10.1007/978-3-030-73081-9_5

xiongdi). Using a story type popular in Chinese cinema, *chuanyue* (time travel), the film features Huang encountering his youthful, hopeful self. The *Crazy Stone* phenomenon is now a twelve-year-old memory, but the established Huang, an award-winning, iconic film actor, feels the need to retrieve his youthful daring—or call it craziness—to remove the doldrums and fear in his career. "You need to move forward! If you don't start, you never know your potential," the 1994 Huang encourages him while the two share a bucket of chicken backstage at a pop concert. *Crazy Twins* is set in the year when former popstar Huang moved to Beijing, turning from a pop singer into a film actor. Acknowledging the youthful advice from his earlier self to follow his heart (accompanied by one of his old hit songs about a tiny bird seeking the expanse of sky), adult Huang confirms he needs to become a film director to better express himself. Huang's unique way of boosting his courage testifies to what we discussed in the introduction of this study that the impact of *Crazy Stone* on Chinese cinema is much like what *Pulp Fiction* did to shake up "a tired, bloated movie industry" in the West, and in using disreputable characters to make unique, interesting, and marketable films (Siskel and Ebert 1995). To be crazy, as this retrieval indicates, is to rejuvenate (Fig. 5.1).

Huang went from a supporting actor in *Crazy Stone* (2006) to the male lead in *Crazy Racer* (2009) and, in between, won the Best Actor award at Taiwan's the 46th Golden Horse Awards with his lead role in the noir comedy *Cow* (Dou niu, 2009). Huang established himself as an icon in contemporary Chinese film and popular culture with the unmistakably dark, clownish craziness he portrays in these films. His character type also

Fig. 5.1   *Crazy Twins.* To be crazy is to rejuvenate

delineates the features of noir films investigated in this study, anti-heroes who are not particularly attractive to start with. The character is often from the grassroots and a member of low life. The craziness in the story is often due to existential absurdity, some desperation, and the character's lack of control over his own fate. The postmodern narrative flair, that is, the film-culture-nourished, *egao*-driven mischief in storytelling, often contributes to the urgency for the character to respond in a carnival-like situation, further heightening the sense of chaos.

Some considered this mini film Huang Bo's advertisement for his directing debut, *The Island* (Yichu haoxi), which came out in August of the same year. The film is an allegorical exploration of human nature and social formation within a story of survival: a man discovers he has won a lottery jackpot at the very moment a catastrophe leaves him and his co-workers shipwrecked on a wild island, turning their team-building exercise into a series of shifting alliances to better survive the primitive conditions. Interesting enough, this film offers not only another example of neo-noir comedy studied in this book but also testifies to the potential of this type of film to succeed in the international market. Admittedly, most of the films we have studied in this book, primarily due to their connection with *egao* culture, are meant for China's domestic market, and there has been less opportunity to envision their cross-cultural reception. In comparison to Zhang Yimou's *A Simple Noodle Story,* which received a 32 percent "freshness rating" on rottentomatoes.com, *The Island* received a 100 percent rating according to critics and an 82 percent rating according to audiences. The thrust created by China's cinematic craziness is obviously appreciated. "China's Latest Mega-Hit," one American critic exclaims, "proves that American comedies are playing things too safe" (Ehrlich 2018). The film's noir feel is also captured. "The psychological dynamics of social interaction," critic Frank Ochieng remarks, "are sardonically at play in the skillful survivalist black comedy."[1] The fact that the film is not a parody of a known Western work but can immediately suggest one appears to be beneficial. While Zhang's parody of *Blood Simple* tends to confuse Western audiences, the similarity of Huang's film to *Lord of the Flies* actually helps.

The second retrieval of the cinematic craziness occurred a year later, also in the Chinese New Year season, when film director Ning Hao finally made his crazy-titled films a trilogy by releasing *Crazy Alien* (Fengkuang de waixing ren, 2019). The anticipation lasted a long time: Ning spent five years working on the script before he could hold a press conference in

2017 to announce his "return to craziness." The post-production of the film, in addition, took longer than a year. For the first two installments of the trilogy, with their small budgets and enormous box office success, Ning had become an advocate for small-to-medium-budget films, and he was even encouraged by film critics to produce a Ning Hao brand for film marketing. Ning directed three films between the second and third installments of the crazy trilogy: *Guns and Roses* (Huanjin da jiean, 2012)—an absurd historical comedy; *No Man's Land* (Wu ren qu, 2013)—a grim, noir Chinese Western road film; and *Breakup Buddies* (Xin hua lu fang, 2014)—a humorous road trip romance. With his brand building in mind, Ning has created the expectation for good storytelling specifically tailored to the genre. Knowing this expectation, one better understands his five years' fine-tuning of the script for *Crazy Alien*; he is a firm believer that the success of a film depends primarily on telling the story well. Although *Guns and Roses* caused disappointment when Ning abandoned the multiple-story-line narrative, there were also fans who just loved how he narrated a historical drama, a blockbuster, with a peculiar grassroots flavor. *Crazy Alien* retains this peculiarity. It is not a low/medium-budget film. Ning's success has skyrocketed its investment figure to about 2.8 billion RMB. The film's low-budget feel, nonetheless, is unmistakable. Even without a multiple-story-line narrative, Ning does not lose the game-like vigor in telling his stories, and he has, as he did with the previous two installments of the trilogy, found for his story a MacGuffin, that is, the plot device that motivates the characters, advances the story, and anchors the allegories.

Whereas Ning never complains about the time spent on the script, he dislikes the post-production sojourn, which often disqualifies his sense of being an auteur. The example he gives is that it takes an artist to work out a normal-sized sculpture, but it takes an engineer to work out an identical sculpture many times larger than that (Zhang Wei 2019). To produce *Crazy Alien*, Ning had funding and resources available to make his film in Hollywood style. He had Joel Hynek, the well-known visual effects artist, signed on to work with him, and he employed four internationally ranked special effect companies (TAU Films, TIPPETT, BUF, and OBLIQUE FX). Yet in the long post-production period, what he thought of most was how he would not let the high-tech elements of the film remove him from the Chinese grassroots and how he would insert his auteur impact by Sinicizing his story world (Zhang Wei 2019). What inspires him is still the *egao* playfulness. He knows the audience will be thinking of *E.T.* while watching *Crazy Alien,* and he hopes the effect of doing so is like seeing Leonardo da Vinci's *Mona Lisa* vis-à-vis Marcel Duchamp's *L.H.O.O.Q.*

In *Crazy Alien*, the monkey performance at a Chinese world park (a theme park with miniature replicas of famous monuments from across globe) is disrupted for a struggling trainer (played by Huang Bo) after an alien crash-lands on Earth and injures his monkey. Desperate to continue to perform the act, he and his liquor-dealer friend mistake the alien as another type of monkey and attempt to train him to perform tricks ranging from riding a bicycle to saluting visitors. The crash is caused by an Amerikan astronaut, who makes first contact with the alien—but ruins Earth's initial attempt at diplomacy by triggering a camera flash for a selfie that shocks and disorients the alien's vehicle.[2] The alien, temporarily separated from his headband (which gives him speech and superb physical power but is taken by the unaware monkey trainer), has to stay in slavery under harsh training but also turns Dionysian, a creature having fallen in love with the Chinese strong liquor, *baijiu.* Hilarious drunken acts are performed with possession of the headband shifting between the trainer and the alien. In the meantime, Amerikans try to recapture the alien to save the disrupted diplomacy. Their efforts, however, become part of the "circus show" choreographed by the trainer and the alien.

The headband is the MacGuffin of the story. For Chinese audiences, it is a familiar device in the Monkey King legend, best represented in the classical novel *Xiyou ji* (Journey to the West). In this intricate but most popular novel of allegories, there are two quests. The first is the monkey's personal search for power and longevity that leads not only to his conflict with the Jade Emperor but also eventually to his being imprisoned by Buddha in the Five-Pillar Mountains (that can easily be interpreted as five essential elements of nature). The second quest involves the monkey's joining other disciples of a Tang Dynasty monk to form a group of five (five essential elements again to formulate the totality of a human being) in the collective search of Buddhist truth and enlightenment. In relation to allegories, whereas the monk represents ordinary human beings, the monkey configures a human's restless ambition. A band is installed on the monkey's head for the second quest; it means to curb his tendency for rash actions so that he may better merge into the quest for the Buddhist truth.

In this film of *egao*, the headband is not for control but for empowerment, and it helps build a big, anti-hegemony irony of jest. The alien starts with the arrogant slur at the beginning of the film that the assignment to communicate with a "filthy planet" disgusts him, and he dislikes the protocol of the "low life form." With this attitude, his contact with the most powerful establishment on the Earth, represented by Amerikan government, can only become confrontational. Ironically, when the alien's vehicle crashes, he himself is turned into a lower life form—mistaken as a monkey and forced into circus performing. The end of his slavery depends on regaining the headband. Temporarily possessing the band allows him to send snapshots of his location as SOS messages, which when intercepted by Amerikans only mislead them to the real locations of those theme park replicas. When the alien first regains the headband and accuses his abusers, they offer him liquor along with the common philosophy that a drink equals an apology and that liquor can resolve all confrontation. He becomes drunk and is captured again, this time soaked in a large container of liquor like a piece of pickle. The Amerikans find his place of capture at this moment. His captors, relying on a trainer's wisdom, dress their real monkey as the alien and conduct a circus show of "the alien" to accept the gene sample from the Amerikans. In the chaos of the Amerikan discovery of the swindle and the capturers' effort to bury the alien, the alien controls the headband and the real monkey. Here the film presents the concluding passage that recalls the episode of the Monkey King raising havoc against Heaven in *Xiyou ji*, but all in irony—the possessed real monkey (abuser and abused in one) denounces human beings (both the lower orders and the establishment but generally accused by the alien as an "inferior civilization" that "does not deserve to exist"). The alien eventually collects a gene sample of the "stupid monkey guy" and bids his farewell to the Earth in a way that shows that he has been contaminated by liquor philosophy— "[let's forget about confrontations and] seek all in [the oblivion of] the liquor!"

In this comedic story, typical Hollywood heroes that the film parodies are devoured by a collective culture which is not praised but portrayed as existentially omnipresent and contaminating. Known in China as "soy-sauce-jar culture" (jianggang wenhua), the term is coined for cultural critique, mocking "a confused society in which the forces of erosion and the forces of stagnation are at their most powerful" and warning of "politics of enslavement."[3] Just like the alien in the film is literally soaked in a similar jar, the Chinese mock themselves for being soaked in a cultural jar showing accumulative erosive effect of long history that is hard to define but also hard to be rid of, not glorious to talk about but practical to use. In a Dionysian irony, the film offers the effect of this culture trait as a solution to contemporary global conflicts in reference to Samuel Huntington's

The Clash of Civilizations. Ning calls his hilarious cinematic comment on global conflicts "postmodern." According to him, the film is not telling a happy-ever-after kind of fairytale but, in "postmodernism or absurdity," "reaches for an alternative truth that the nature of the world has no particular order; there is nothing in this world that can be fundamentally solved by egotism of the human beings" (Zhang Wei 2019, 101).

Ning's use of postmodernism vindicates the term's popularity in this round of cinematic craziness, not only among scholars but also among artists and the general audience in the sense of irony, playfulness, and absurdity. As discussed in the book, the Chinese use of postmodernism and the Western concept of postmodernism are responses to differed cultural, social, and historical elements. They, nonetheless, show a striking similarity in representation. *Crazy Alien*'s example coincides with how Linda Hutcheon, a Canadian scholar on postmodernism, describes postmodern parody, that is, to quote a convention for the sake of jeering at it, and this representation "takes the form of self-conscious, self-contradictory, self-undermining statement" (2002, 1).

Some misunderstand *Crazy Alien* as nationalist, anti-American propaganda since it makes American agents and government the central object of ridicule. The film may indeed be a response to the contemporary, escalating Neo-Cold War (trade war included) between China and the United States, but it is also an *egao* parody of Hollywood's portrayal of American establishments. The caricature of the Americans is primarily for the sake of building a postmodern, Chinese self-mockery. What deconstructs global hegemony is the winning of the soy-sauce-jar culture, and there is much absurdity, bitterness, and ridicule in its win.

When *Crazy Stone* first came out, Chinese scholars hailed it as the proof of the validity of postmodernism in China. A dozen plus years down the road, postmodernism is still in vogue in Ning's return to cinematic craziness. It so happens that postmodernism helps spell out some essential narrative features of this round of neo-noir craziness: the ironies are tongue-in-cheek, *egao* renders much as quoted materials of parody, playfulness is existentially situated (primarily in stories about the grassroots) to push for the sense of absurdity, and lack of confidence produces a sense of darkness.

Looking at the two retrievals together, I want to highlight the monkey image in this round of cinematic craziness. In the introduction to this book, while surveying historical configuration of craziness, we focused on the etymological implications of dog challenging the king, reinforced by both Foucault's discussion of dog image in relation to cynicism and the Chinese coinage of cynicism as "dog Confucianism." Whereas this dog image is most enlightening for an understanding of craziness, it will fail a popularity test with the rival image of the monkey, particularly as maintained by the Monkey King legend, which enacts carnival—a mass revelry that connects both popular and high culture. Ning Hao testifies to the strong impact of the Monkey King in his manufacturing of cinematic craziness (Fig. 5.2). In 2012, Ning first named his own film studio Dirty Monkey (*huai houzi*) and then, on the 10th anniversary of *Crazy Stone*, announced a most ambitious film production program known as "72 Transformations of Dirty Monkey." *Crazy Alien* is the first film the program publicized, and then ten emerging film directors signed on to the program with their films. Among these directors, Wen Muye's 2018 film *Dying to Survive* (Wo bushi yaoshen) and Shen Ao's 2019 film *My Dear Liar* (Shouyi ren) both became critically acclaimed and popular, furthering the impact of neo-noir comedies studied in this book. "From one dirty monkey to a group of dirty monkeys," Ning reflects, "we hope to represent 'us'" (Chen Xiaonao 2017). Obviously, Ning is using his "brand" of films to attract investment to help younger directors with kindred pursuits to emerge. In a way, what he hopes for is brand recognition, similar to what viewers would expect for the films produced by Plan B Entertainment and A24 in America. In 2006, Andy Lau's "New Star Directors of Asia" program jump-started the careers of both Ning Hao and Huang Bo. It is not coincidental that both of them are doing similar things for the

Fig. 5.2 *Crazy Alien*. A monkey story

forthcoming, even younger artists in their fields—Ning Hao with the program of "72 Transformations of Dirty Monkey" and Huang Bo with "HB+U: Youth Directors Support Program." While promoting these programs, both artists retrieve cinematic craziness, and the Monkey King image accompanies them in doing so. Huang Bo's *Crazy Twins* showcases him confronting a Monkey King performer at a marketplace, drawing inspiration from this icon. Ning Hao's *Crazy Alien* relies heavily on the monkey image, which leads the director to reflect, "The mischievous monkey is a sign in our culture. It is that of a critique of mainstream culture" (Zhang Wei 2019, 98).

Notes

1. Frank Ochieng is one of the nine critics quoted by the website *Rotten Tomatoes* in rating *The Island*. https://www.rottentomatoes.com/m/the_island_2018 (accessed May 21, 2019).
2. The film's fictional *C Guo* (C Country) refers to the United States of America. The English subtitle of the film translates it into "Amerika."
3. Although Ning Hao is not referring to him but to Yang Jiang's use of it, Taiwanese cultural critic Bo Yang is the person who focused popular attention on the "soy-sauce-jar culture." The title of Bo's most controversial book of 1985, *The Ugly Chinaman*, speaks for his approach of self-mockery. The quote from Bo here is taken from Wei Ming Dariotis and Eileen Fung, "Breaking the Soy Sauce Jar: Diaspora and Displacement in the Films of Ang Lee" in Sheldon Hsiao-peng Lu, ed. *Transnational Chinese Cinemas: Identity, Nationhood, Gender* (University of Hawai'i Press, 1997), 187.

References

Chinese Language Sources

Chen Xiaonao. 2017. Huai houzi gongbu piandan: Ning Hao chongqi fengkuang xilie (Dirty Monkeys Publicize Film List: Ning Hao Reinitiate Crazy Series). Film News, Tengxun entertainment, posted June 20, 2017. http://ent.qq.com/a/20170620/010300.htm. Accessed 19 Jan 2019.
Zhang Wei. 2019. *Fengkuang de waixing ren*: chuangzao zhongguo dianying de dute secai: Ninghao fangtan (Creating Idiosyncrasy in Chinese Film: An Interview with Ning Hao on *Crazy Alien*). *Dianying yishu* (Film Arts) 2: 97–102.

English Language Sources

Ehrlich, David. 2018. 'The Island' Review: China's Latest Mega-Hit Proves that American Comedies Are Playing Things Too Safe. Posted Aug 24, 2018. https://www.indiewire.com/2018/08/the-island-review-huang-bo-shu-qi-1201997399/. Accessed 21 May 2019.

Hutcheon, Linda. 2002. *The Politics of Postmodernism.* 2nd ed. London/New York: Routledge.

Siskel, Gene, and Roger Ebert. 1995. Pulp Faction: The Tarantino Generation. *Pulp Fiction* DVD. Burbank: Buena Vista Home Entertainment.

Ning Hao

Crazy Stone (Fengkuang de shitou, 2006)
Crazy Racer/Silver Medalist (Fengkuang de saiche, 2009)

REFERENCES

CHINESE LANGUAGE SOURCES

Anon. 2005. Q ban wenhua si da yuanliu (Four Major Sources of Q Version Culture), posted March 15, 2005. http://www.chinanews.com.cn/news/2005/2005_03_15/26/550622.shtml. Accessed June 5, 2014.

———. 2010. Daoyan Ah Gan de ziliao (Data About Director Ah Gump), posted February 26, 2010. http://zhidao.baidu.com/question/139379217.html. Accessed 10 May 2012.

Chai Xiaofeng. 1989. Huashuo *fengkuang de daijia*: yu zhou xiaowen duihua lu (Concerning *Obsession*: A Dialogue with Zhou Xiaowen). *Dangdai dianying* (Contemporary Cinema) 2: 75–84.

———, ed. 1996. *Zhou Xiaowen: Xiaowen ye fengkuang* (Zhou Xiaowen: Xiaowen Is Equally Crazy). Changsha: Hunan wenyi chubanshe.

Chang Fangfei. 2018. Ning Hao xunzhao Ning Hao (Ning Hao in Search of Ning Hao). Huxiu.com, posted July 15, 2018. https://baijiahao.baidu.com/s?id=1606012633168373921&wfr=spider&for=pc. Accessed 16 Dec 2018.

Chang Qing. 2008. Wulitou: yizhong liuxing de dazhong wenhua xianxiang (*Wulitou*: A Trendy Mass Culture Phenomenon). *Shandong shifan daxue xuebao* (Journal of Shandong Normal University—Humanities and Social Sciences edition) 3: 71–75.

Chen Dianlin. 2009. Shanzhai wenhua: dikang yu yiyu (Shanzhai Culture: Resistance and Ridicule). *Xueshu tansuo* (Academic Exploration) 1: 107–110.

Chen Hongxiu. 2012. Heise youmo yu zhongguo dalu xiju dianying: jianlun heise youmo pian yu heise xiju pian de yitong (Black Humor Films and Chinese

© The Author(s), under exclusive license to Springer Nature Switzerland AG 2021
H. H. Kuoshu, *Craziness and Carnival in Neo-Noir Chinese Cinema*, Chinese Literature and Culture in the World, https://doi.org/10.1007/978-3-030-73081-9

Mainland Comic Films: Also on the Difference Between Black Humor and Dark Comedy Films). *Qinghai shehui kexue* (Qinghai Journal of Social Sciences) 2: 177–180.

Chen Jie. 2010. Ning Hao de leixing yu yiyi (Ning Hao's Genre and Implications). *Beijing dianying xueyuan xuebao* (Journal of Beijing Film Academy) 2: 41–46.

Chen Linxia. 2006. Egao de xiju: dangxia dianying yishu de shangyehua silu yu xianjing (*Egao* Comedy: Orientations and Traps in Commercialization of Contemporary Film Arts). *Qilu yiyuan* (Journal of Shandong Arts Academy) 6: 37–42.

———. 2010. *Sanqiang paian jingji* yu san ge beilun (*A Simple Noodle Story* and Three Paradoxes). *Yishu guangjiao* (Art Panorama) 2: 46–50.

Chen Mo. 2010. Wo kan *sanqiang pai'an jingqi* (My View on *A Simple Noodle Story*). *Dangdai dianying* (Contemporary Cinema) 2: 34–36.

Chen Xi. 2011. Shilun dangdai yujing xia houxiandai hese youmo xiju de xushi celue (On Narratives of Post-Modern, Black-Humor Comedies in Contemporary Discourses). *Dianying pingjie* (Movie Reviews) 12: 1–3.

Chen Xiaoming. 1993. *Wubian de tiaozhan: Zhongguo xianfeng wenxue de houxiandai xing* (Borderless Challenge: The Postmodern Features of Chinese Avant-Garde Literature). Beijing: Beijing University Press.

Chen Xiaonao. 2017. Huai houzi gongbu piandan: Ning Hao chongqi fengkuang xilie (Dirty Monkeys Publicize Film List: Ning Hao Reinitiate Crazy Series). Film News, Tengxun entertainment, posted June 20, 2017. http://ent.qq.com/a/20170620/010300.htm. Accessed 19 Jan 2019.

Chen Yan. 2006. Xiandai yujing xia de dianying shuxie: ping guochan dianying *fengkuang de shitou* (Film Writing in Contemporary Context of Discourses: A Discussion of Domestic Film *Crazy Stone*). *Dianying pingjie* (Movie Review) 21: 30–32.

Dong Dingshan. 1980. Suowei houxiandai pai xiaoshuo (The So-Called Postmodern Fiction). *Dushu* (Book Review) 12: 135–139.

Du Jinyan. 2006. Q ban: jiti moqi de ya wenhua (Q version: A Collectively-Agreed Subculture). *Qingnian yanjiu* (Youth Studies) 9: 10–15.

Fan Fangjun. 2006. Cong jiegou dao jiangou: ershi nian houxiandai zhuyi zai zhongguo de jieshou shiping (From Deconstruction to Construction: A Discussion of Twenty Years of Reception of Postmodernism in China). *Wenyi lilun yu piping* (Literary Theory and Criticism) 1: 123–127.

Fang Zhou. 2007. Zhou Xiaowen koushu: 'Fengkuang'de dianying shidai (Zhou Xiaowen Testimony: Crazy Era of Film Production). *Dazhong dianying* (Popular Cinema) 21: 42–45.

Ge Hua. 1994. Mimang zhi lu: chongdu Zhou Xiaowen (A Journey of Confusion: Reread Zhou Xiaowen). *Dangdai dianying* (Contemporary Cinema) 5: 37–44.

Gong Changyu. 2002. Ku wenhua mantan (Random Discussion of Ku Culture). *Daode yu wenming* (Ethics and Civilization) 2: 71–75.

Gong Jie. 2007. Houxiandai yujing xia de kuanghuan hua xushu (Carnival Narrative in the Discursive Context of Postmodernity). *Dianying pingjie* (Movie Review) 4: 33–34 and 37.

Guo Cen. 2009. Lun *fengkuang de saiche* xushi fengge (On the Narrative Style of *Crazy Racer*). *Dianying wenxue* (Film Literature) 19: 70–71.

Hao Jian. 2002. Xushi kuanghuan he guaixiao de heise: haolaiwu guaicai kunting talandino chuangzuo lun (The Carnival Narration and the Darkness of Bizarre Laughter: On Film Arts of Hollywood Weird Genius Quentin Tarantino). *Dangdai dianying* (Contemporary Cinema) 1: 59–68.

He Lei. 2015. Lun dangdai zhongguo dazhong wenhua jiazhi xuwuzhuyi de quxiang lujing (On Orientations of Value Nihilism in Today's Chinese Mass Culture). *Dangdai wentan* (Contemporary Literary Platform) 3: 146–150.

He Ping, et al. 2005. Dangxia wenxue zhong de xiaozi qingdiao he zhongchan jieji quwei (Petty-Bourgeois Sensibility and Middle Class Taste in Contemporary Literature). *Wenyi pinglun* (Literature and Art Criticism) 6: 50–55.

Hong Xiaonan, and Li Yan. 2010. Houxiandai zhuyi dui zhongguo daxuesheng ku wenhua de yingxiang (Postmodern Impact on Chinese College Students' *Ku* Culture). *Dalian ligong daxue xuebao* (Journal of Dalian University of Technology—Social Sciences Edition) 31 (2): 35–39.

Hu Puzhong. 2008. *Wo jiao liu yuejin*: shangye hua de jieji biaoda (*Lost and Found*: Commercialized Social Class Representation). *Dianying yishu* (Film Arts) 3: 55–57.

Jiang Tianping, and Xia Yiqun. 2007. Huangdan de shengyan, hou xiandai de kuanghuan: lun *fengkuang de shitou* de houxiandai tezheng (Absurd Banquet, Postmodern Carnival: On the Postmodern Characteristics of *Crazy Stone*). *Dangdai wentan* (Contemporary Literary Platform) 2: 149–151.

Lao Yang. 2009. Duihua daoyan A Gan (A Dialogue with Director Ah Gump), posted February 18, 2009. http://i.mtime.com/646748/blog/1692122/. Accessed 10 May 2012.

Li Fengliang. 2001. Jieshou Kundela: jiedu yu wudu (Kundera Reception: Reading and Misreading). *Guowai wenxue* (Foreign Literature) 81–82: 58–69.

Li Huoxiu. 2010. Yiyi de queshi yu jiangou: xiaofei wenhua yujing xia zhongguo shanzhai dianying fazhan xianzhuang de fansi (Absence and Construct of Meanings: Reflection on Chinese *Shanzhai* Films in the Context of Commercial Culture). *Dangdai dianying* (Contemporary Cinema) 2: 155–158.

Li Lingling. 2009. Shanzhai wenhua: web2.0 shidai de caogen kuanghuan (*Shanzhai* Culture: Grassroots Carnival in the Era of Web2.0). *Xinwen jie* (News Media) 1: 108–110.

Li Shengtao. 2007. *Fengkuang de shitou* daodi fanfeng le shenme? (What Does *Crazy Stone* Jeer at After All?). *Dianying pingjie* (Movie Review) 12: 51–52.

Li Xiaofei. 2009. Shanzhai wenhua de sikao (Contemplation of *Shanzhai* Culture). *Xinwen jie* (News Media) 2: 124–126.

Li Yang. 2008. Youxi: liudong de xiandaixing (Game: Modernity in Fluidity). *Yishu pinglun* (Art Review) 3: 54–56.

Li Yiming. 1989. Shifu xingwei zhi hou: dangdai dianying zhong de jiating queshi yu buchang (With Fathers Being Slain: The Loss of Families and Its Compensation in Contemporary Chinese Films). *Dianying yishu* (Film Arts) 6: 9–18.

Li Yunlei. 2009. Women weishenme er jiang gushi: cong *fengkuang de saiche* shuoqi (Why Do We Tell Stories: With *Crazy Racer* as a Point of Departure for Discussion). *Dianying yishu* (Film Arts) 2: 18–20.

———. 2013. Xin xiaozi de dichenghua yu wenhua lingdaoquan wenti (New Petty Bourgeoisie's Touch with Lower Depth and the Issue of Cultural Leadership). *Nanfang wentan* (Southern Literary Platform) 1: 39–41.

Li Zehou. 2008. *Zhongguo xiandai sixiangshi lun* (On Contemporary Chinese Intellectual History). Beijing: Sanlian shudian.

Liu Xueming. 2007. Dazhong wenhua yu houxiandaizhuyi de ronghe: jianxi *fengkuang de shitou* de hou xiandai zhuyi tezheng (The Merge of Mass Culture and Postmodernism: A Brief Analysis of Postmodern Features of *Crazy Stone*). *Dianying pingjie* (Movie Review) 6: 33–34.

Liu Yibin. 2007. Mo zhe 'fengkuang de shitou' guohe (Cross the River by the Foothold Guidance of "Crazy Stones"). *Dianying yishu* (Film Arts) 3: 76–78.

Liu Zhongze. 2013. Wangluo minzu zhuyi gainian bianxi (An Analysis of the Concept of Net Nationalism). *Beijing qingnian zhengzhi xueyuan xuebao* (Journal of Beijing Academy of Political Science) 1: 37–41.

Lu Daofu. 2002. Kuanghuan lilun yu yuehan feisike de dazhong wenhua yanjiu (Carnival Theory and John Fiske's Research on Popular Culture). *Waiguo wenxue yanjiu* (Foreign Literature Research) 4: 21–27 and 154.

———. 2003. Yuehan feisike dazhong wenhua lilun yanjiu shuping (A Survey of the Research on John Fiske's Popular Culture Theory). *Xueshu yanjiu* (Scholarly Research) 1: 100–104.

Luo Luo. 2006. *Wulin waizhuan*: xinue wuxia er bu dianfu xiayi (*My Own Swordsman*: Teasing but not Undermining Martial Arts). *Nanqiang beidiao* (Accents North and South) 4: 11–12.

Luo Xuehui. 2005. fennen fennen de Q ban shenghuo: dushiren ziwo jianya de jiti moqi (Powdered, Tender Q Version Life: Metropolitans' Consensus on Releasing Tension). *Xiandai jiaoji* (Contemporary Communication) 9: 10.

Ma Liwen, and Wu Quanping. 2008. Ta jiao Liu Yuejing: Ma Liwen fangtan (About Film *Lost and Found*: An Interview of Ma Liwen). *Dianying yishu* (Film Arts) 2: 76–79.

Meng Fanxuan. 2014. *Bairi yanhuo*: zhongguo heise dianying tansuo daolu de shuguang (*Black Coal, Thin Ice*: The Dawn of China's Research of Film Noir). *Jin tian* (Golden Field) 299: 123–124.

Ning Hao, and Wu Quanping. 2009. Jiang gushi shi yimen jishu huo—Ning Hao fangtan (Film Stories Are Told by Techniques—An Interview with Ning Hao). *Dianying yishu* (Film Arts) 2: 72–77.

Quang Tenglong. 2011. Gai Liqi, Ning Hao dianying sheying jiaodu de bijiao jiexi (A Comparative Analysis of Shooting Angles Used by Guy Richee and Ning Hao). *Dianying pingjie* (Movie Review) 15: 6–8.

Rong Weiqian. 1994. Zhou Xiaowen: bei dianying kesi de daoyan (Zhou Xiaowen: A Dead-Serious Director About Films). *Dianying yishu* (Film Arts) 5: 45–49.

Shi Yonggang, and Liu Qiongxiong. 2006. *Zhou Xingchi ying hua* (Stephen Chow Motion Pictures). Beijing: Zuojia chubanshe.

Sha Dan. 2009. Xiaofei huangdan: wanjin zhongguo heise xiju de moshi yu bianxi (To Consume Absurdity: Analyzing the Modes of Recent Black Comedy). *Dianying yishu* (Film Arts) 6: 67–71.

Song Juan, and Wang Mingfeng. 2009. Jiang 'kuanghuan' jinxing daodi (Carry the Carnival to the End). *Anhui wenxue* (Anhui Literature) 2: 374.

Song Xiaojun, et al. 2009. *Zhongguo bugaoxing* (Unhappy China: The Great Time, Grand Vision and Our Challenges). Nanjing: Jiangsu renmin chubanshe.

Tao Dongfeng, et al. 2005. Guanyu *Q ban yuwen* yu dahua wenhua xianxiang de taolun (A Discussion About *Q version Chinese* and *wulitou* Culture). *Dangdai wentan* (Contemporary Literary Platform) 3: 50–53.

Tao Dongfeng. 2009. Wuliao, shale, shanzhai: lijie dangxia jingshen wenhua de guanjianci (Boredom, Silly Laughter, Rebels' Camp: Key Phrases for Understanding Contemporary Ethical Culture). *Dangdai wentan* (Contemporary Literary Platform) 4: 9–12.

Wang Chao. 2009. Dianying shoufa de bentuhua: *fengkuang de shitou* yu gai liqi de ying pian de bijiao fenxi (Local Application of Film Skills: A Comparison of *Crazy Stone* and Guy Richy Films). *Dianying pingjie* (Movie Review) 1: 51–52.

Wang Di. 2009. Dianying *fengkuang de shitou* zhi jiegou celue (Deconstructive Strategies in *Crazy Stone*). *Zuojia zazhi* (Writers) 8: 201–202.

Wang Guojie. 2009. Xifang: chaoyue egao de pingminhua yishu (Parody: A Plebian Art That Transcends *Egao*). *Dianying wenxue* (Film Literature) 5: 14–15.

Wang Hongtu. 2007. Kundela re yu wenhua quanru zhuyi (Milan Kundera Fad and Cultural Cynicism). *Tansuo yu zhengming* (Exploration and Debate) 3: 28–31.

Wang Li. 2009. Zhuolue mofang haishi chuangzaoxing jiegou: houxiandai zhuyi guanzhao xia de wangluo e'gao (Cheap Imitation or Creative Deconstruction: Internet *Egao* Considered in Postmodern Perspective). *Kejiao wenhui* (Science and Education Digest) 5: 228 and 233.

Wang Ning. 1993. *Duoyuan gongsheng de shidai* (An Era of Multiplicity). Beijing: Beijing daxue chubanshe.

Wang Shuo. 2004. *Wang Shuo wenji: suibi ji* (Works of Wang Shuo: Essays). Kunming: Yunnan renmin chuban she.

Wang Wenbin. 2009. Fengkuang yijiu, zhenshi bu zai: dui dianying *fengkuang saiche* de pipanxing kaocha (Madness Continues, Reality No More: A Critical Investigation of *Crazy Racing Car*). *Lilun yu chuangzuo* (Criticism and Creation) 128 (3): 102–104.

———. 2013. Cong caogen kuanghuan dao jiaguo xushi: lun ning hao shangye dianying de muti chengzhang yu leixing jiaolu (From Grassroots Carnival to Family and National Narrative: On Archetypes in Ning Hao's Commercial Films and Anxiety in Coming of Age). *Beijing dianying xueyuan xuebao* (Journal of Beijing Film Academy) 1: 47–50.

Wang Wenzhong, et al. 2006. Dianying *fengkuang de shitou*: yici chenggong de shangyepian tuwei (Film *Crazy Stone*: A Breakthrough from Commercial Films). *Dianying pingjie* (Movie Review) 22: 29–30.

Wang Xueqian. 2010. Lu Xun de 'fengkuang' xushi yu daojia wenhua (Lu Xun's 'Crazy' Narrative and Taoism). *Jilin shifan daxue xuebao* (Journal of Jilin Normal University) 6: 5–8.

Wang Yang. 2005. Hou xiandai zhuyi zai zhongguo (Postmodernism in China). *Shehui kexue luntan* (Social Sciences Platform) 1: 149–152.

Wang Yichuan. 2003. Zhongguo dianying de hou qinggan shidai: *yingxiong* qishi lu (Era of Post-Emotionalism in Chinese Film Production: Ideas Inspired by the Film *Hero*). *Dangdai dianying* (Contemporary Cinema) 2: 16–18.

———. 2004. Cong qinggan zhuyi dao hou qinggan zhuyi (From Emotionalism to Post-Emotionalism). *Wenyi zhengming* (Arts Forum) 1: 6–9.

Wang Ying. 2004. Hou xiandai fenwei xia de lundun gushi (A London Story in Postmodern Aura). *Beijing dianying xueyuan xuebao* (Journal of Beijing Film Academy) 5: 51–56.

Wang Yuechuan. 2001. Hou xiandai hou zhimin zhuyi zai zhongguo (Postmodern and Post-Colonialism in China). *Jiangsu xingzheng xueyuan xuebao* (Journal of Jiansu University of Administration) 1: 119–125, 136.

Wang Zhihong, and Zhu Shiqun. 2012. Dui zhongguo dangdai xuwuzhuyi sichao de zhexue sikao (A Philosophical Consideration of Contemporary Trends of Nihilism in China). *Hebei xuekan* (Hebei Academic Journal) 32 (2): 25–30.

Wu Guanping, et al. 2006. *Fengkuang de shitou*: hese de kuanghuan (*Crazy Stone*: Dark Carnival). *Dianying yishu* (Film Arts) 5: 73–75.

Wu Guanping. 2010. Wanluo wenhua yu kuaican dianying: Wang Yuelun fantan (Web Culture and Fast-Food Film: An Interview of Wang Yuelun). *Dianying yishu* (Film Arts) 2: 89–94.

Xi Yongfeng. 2006. *Fengkuang de shitou*: heise youmo yu kunhuo rensheng (*Crazy Stone*: Black Humor and Puzzling Life). *Dianying wenxue* (Film Literature) 10: 3–6.

Xiu Ti. 2005. Dangdai zhongguo dianying zhong de heise youmo (Black Humor in Contemporary Chinese Film). *Dianying yishu* (Film Arts) 1: 118–121

Xu Ben. 2014. Dangdai quanruzhuyi de liangxin yu xiwang (Conscience and Hope in Contemporary Cynicism). *Dushu* (Book Review) 7: 29–37.

Xu Denan. 2003. Lun Du Fu shi zhong de kuanggu, kuang zou he kuangben (On the Three Madness in Du Fu's Poetry). *Du Fu yanjiu xuekan* (Du Fu Studies Journal) 76 (2): 21–27.

Xu Gang, and Hao Chaoshuai. 2011. 'Diankuang' de zhenghou yu 'gangwei' de zong ji (Symptoms of Craziness and Traces of Hong Kong Flavor). *Beijing dianying xueyuan xuebao* (Journal of Beijing Film Academy) 3: 2–6.

Xu Le. 2006. *Heibai senlin*: xiang gang hei shehui pian de shehui wenhua zheng-hou dujie (*Color of the Truth*: A Reading of Social and Cultural Symptoms of Hong Kong's Black Society Films). *Dianying yishu* (Film Arts) 4: 5–10.

———. 2015. Xianggang jingfeipian de xiandaixing sibian ji wenhua bianzou (Modernity Thinking and Changing Cultural Melodies in Hong Kong Gangster and Cop Films). *Dianying yishu* (Film Arts) 4: 51–55.

Xue Min. 1988. Maerkusai de 'aiyu jiefang lun' shuping (On Marcuse's Liberation of *Eros*). *Fudan xuebao, shehui kexue ban* (Fudan University Journal—Social Science Edition) 5: 107–111.

Yang Di. 2010 *Ye dian* yu *fengkuang de saiche* zhi fubi pushe bijiao (A Comparative Study of the Use of Foreshadowing in *One Night in Supermarket* and *Crazy Racer*). *Dianying pingjie* (Movie Review) 1: 38–39.

Yang Xiaobin. 1989. Yishu de aiyu xiangdu: Maerkusai yu shenmei geming (Love Orientation of Arts: Marcuse and a Revolution in Aesthetics). *Shanghai shehui kexueyuan xueshu jikan* (Scholarship Quarterly of Shanghai Academy of Social Sciences) 21 (2): 175–184.

Ye Shuxian. 1999. Zhongguo wenhua zhong de fengkuang (Madness in Chinese Culture). *Xin dongfang* (New East) 1: 40–54.

Yin Hong, and Shi Huimin. 2009. 2008: zhongguo dianying chanye beiwang (2008: A Memorandum of Film Industry). *Dianying yishu* (Film Arts) 2: 5–13.

Yin Kangzhuang. 2010. Wulitou wenhua tanlun (Tentative Comment on *Wulitou* Culture). *Jinan xuebao* (Journal of Jinan University—Philosophy and Social Sciences Edition) 1: 20–26.

Yu Qian, and Zheng Jun. 2012. You *fengkuang de shitou* kan zhongguo houxian-dai dianying fazhan (A Look at Postmodern Film Development in China via *Crazy Stone*). *Dianying wenxue* (Movie Literature) 22: 83–84.

Yu Yingshi. 1987. *Shi yu zhongguo wenhua* (Shi Scholar and Chinese Culture). Shanghai renmin chubanshe.

Yuan Kejia. 1982. Guanyu hou xiandai zhuyi sichao (About Postmodern Trend of Thinking). *Guowai shehui kexue* (Social Sciences Abroad) 11: 28–31.

Yuan Ying, et al. 1989. *Fengkuang de daijia* bitan (Panel Discussion of *Obsession*). *Dangdai dianying* (Contemporary Cinema) 2: 85–94.

Yuan Zushe. 2009. Xuwu zhuyi de wenhua jingxiang yu dangdai zhongguo 'ziwo jingyan' shijian de kunjing (Cultural Mirror of Nihilism and Practical Dilemma of Chinese "Self-Experience"). *Shaanxi shifan daxue xuebao* (Journal of Shaanxi Normal University, Philosophy and Social Sciences Edition) 6: 5–11.

Zeng Jun. 2006. Bahejin kuanghuan hua lilun yu xifang makesi zhuyi (Bakhtin's Carnival Theory and Western Marxism). *Xibei shida xuebao* (Journal of Northwest Normal University) 43 (5): 1–8.

Zhang Guoyun, and Li Hui. 2011. Xiao zhong dai lei de beixi rensheng: wulitou beihou de zhou xingchi diangying (Tragi-Comic Life in Laughter with Tears: Stephen Chow's Films in Light of *wulitou*). *Dangdai dianying* (Contemporary Cinema) 9: 157–160.

Zhang Wei. 2019. *Fengkuang de waixing ren*: chuangzao zhongguo dianying de dute secai: Ninghao fangtan (Creating Idiosyncrasy in Chinese Film: An Interview with Ning Hao on *Crazy Alien*). *Dianying yishu* (Film Arts) 2: 97–102.

———. 2010. 2009 dianying shichang chongdu: 80 hou yu zhongguo dianying meixue (Re-examining 2009 Film Market: Post-80 Generation and Chinese Film Aesthetics). *Beijing dianying xueyuan xuebao* (Journal of Beijing Film Academy) 1: 29–30.

Zhang Xiaoli. 2013. Lun Ning Hao jinqi dianying zhong de heise youmo (On Black Humor in Ning Hao's Recent Films). *Dianying wenxue* (Film Literature) 17: 51–52.

Zhang Xiaomei, et al. 2009. Huangdan de qiaohe, dai xiao de beiliang: Ning Hao 'fengkuang' dianying de shengcunxing tansuo (Absurd Coincidence, Sadness in Laughter: An Existentialist Exploration of Ning Nao's "Crazy" Films). *Neijiang shifan xueyuan xuebao* (Journal of Neijiang Normal University) 24: 51–53.

Zhang Yiwu. 1993. *Zai bianyuan chu zhuisuo: Disan shijie wenhua yu dangdai zhongguo wenxue* (Marginal Inquiries: The Third World Culture and Contemporary Chinese Literature). Beijing: Beijing University Press.

———. 2002. 'Kandie de yi dai' zai jueqi (The Rise of the "Disc-Watching Generation"). *Dangdai dianying* (Contemporary Cinema) 5: 20–21.

———. 2008. Delida he women: zhiji huo moshengren (Derrida and Us: A Bosom Friend or a Stranger), Blogchina, posted July 26, 2008. http://www.blogchina.com/20080726578704.html. Accessed 20 Jan 2011.

———. 2010. *Sanqiang pai'an jingqi*: cong xiju zhong chongxin xunzhao kenengxing (*A Simple Noodle Story*: Rediscovering Possibilities in a Comedy). *Dangdai dianying* (Contemporary Cinema) 2: 27–31.

———. 2013. Hou xiaozi de wenhua xingtai (Cultural Status of Post-Petti-Bourgeoisie). *Zhongguan cun* (Zhongguan Village) 1: 107.

Zhang Yue. 2009. Cong *fengkuang de saiche* kan guochan dianyng de huwen shengchan (*Crazy Racer* and Intertextual Production Among Chinese Films). *Dianying pingjie* (Movie Review) 6: 33 and 35.

Zhang Ziyang. 2004. *Gongfu bufu youxinren: Zhou Xingchi waizhuan* (Where There Is Heart There Is Way: A Biography of Stephen Chow). Beijing: Xinhua chubanshe.

Zhao Yuesheng. 1988. Zou xiang wuyayi wenming: du *aiyu yu wenming* (Towards a Non-Repressive Civilization: Reading *Eros and Civilization*). *Dushu* (Book Review) 8: 12–21.

Zheng Chuangqi. 2005. Hou xin pipingjia: Zhang Yiwu (Post, Neo Critic Zhang Yiwu). *Zhongguan cun* (Zhongguan Village) 22: 30.

Zheng Dongtian, et al. 2006. Xinzuo pingyi: *fengkuang de shitou* (Discussion of New Movies: On *Crazy Stone*). *Dangdai dianying* (Contemporary Cinema) 5: 15–20.

Zheng Dongtian. 2008. Yiqun zhongguo nianqing dianyingren yu yige waiguo zhizhe de shenjiao (The Spiritual Exchange Between a Group of Chinese Young People and a Foreign Wise Man). *Dangdai dianying* (Contemporary Cinema) 4: 4–6.

Zheng Dongtian, et al. 2009. Xinzuo pingyi: *fengkuang de saiche* (Discussion of New Movies: On *Crazy Racer*). *Dangdai dianying* (Contemporary Cinema) 3: 37–44.

Zheng Jian. 2008. Dangdai chuanmei changyu zhong de xiaozi wenhua jiexi (An Analysis of Petti Bourgeois Culture in Contemporary Media). *Dangdai chuanbo* (Contemporary Communication) 1: 49–50.

Zhou Quanxin. 2008. Bosha, zhuizhuo, xiyan: jiti de xixi yu kuanghuan (Killing, Chasing, Teasing: Mass Games and Carnivals). *Dianying wenxue* (Movie Literature) 23: 21–22.

Zhou Yang. 2009. Ning Hao 'fengkuang dianying' de cunzaizhuyi (Existentialism of Ning Hao's Crazy Films). *Shannxi shifan daxue xuebao* (Journal of Shaanxi Normal University—Philosophy and Social Sciences Edition) 38: 380–382.

Zhu Maoqing. 2007. Yuxian zhuangtai xia de kuanghuan yishi (Carnival Rituals in the Liminal Status). *Dianying pinglun* (Movie Review) 10: 27–28.

Zhu Yu. 2010. Cong 'xiandai zhuyi' dao 'wenhua zhengzhi': Zhang Xudong jiaoshou fangtan lu (From "Modernism" to "Cultural Politics": An Interview of Professor Xudong Zhang). *Xiandai zhongwen xuekan* (Journal of Modern Chinese) 3–6: 4–27.

Zou Ping. 2015. Lun dianying *bairi yanhuo* de heise xing he xin tansuo (On the Darkness and New Orientations in the Film *Black Coal, Thin Ice*). *Zhongguo dianying pinglun* (Chinese Movie Review) 17: 24–26.

ENGLISH LANGUAGE SOURCES

Allen, William Rodney. 2006. *The Coen Brothers: Interviews*. Jackson: University Press of Mississippi.

AP. 2010. Sick of All the On-screen Vomiting? posted March 1, 2010. http://www.theage.com.au/news/entertainment/film/articles/2010/03/01/1267291837148.html. Accessed 15 June 2012.

Appadurai, Arjun. 1996. *Modernity at Large: Cultural Dimensions of Globalization*. Minneapolis: University of Minnesota Press.

Bakhtin, M.M. 1984. *Problems of Dostoevsky's Poetics*. Ed. and Trans. Caryl Emerson. Minneapolis/London: University of Minnesota Press.

Barber, Benjamin R. 1996. *Jihad vs. McWorld: How Globalism and Tribalism Are Reshaping the World*. New York: Ballantine Books.

Bell, Daniel. 1976. *The Cultural Contradictions of Capitalism*. New York: Basic Books.

Biber, Douglas. 1988. *Variation Across Speech and Writing*. Cambridge: Cambridge University Press.

Billson, Anne. 2010. Vomit: The Recurring Movie Motif, posted May 6, 2010. http://www.guardian.co.uk/film/2010/may/06/vomit-movie-motif-taboo-billson. Accessed 15 June 2012.

Bordwell, David. 2000. *Planet Hong Kong: Popular Cinema and the Art of Entertainment*. Cambridge, MA/London: Harvard University Press.

Bould, Mark, et al., eds. 2009. *Neo-Noir*. London/New York: Wallflower Press.

Brandt, Stefan L. 2009. The City as Liminal Space: Urban Visuality and Aesthetic Experience in Postmodern US Literature and Cinema. *Amerikastudien/American Studies* 54 (4): 553–581.

Brody, Richard. 2014. 'Film Noir': The Elusive Genre. *The New Yorker*, posted July 23, 2014. http://www.newyorker.com/culture/richard-brody/film-noir-elusive-genre-2. Accessed 25 Feb 2015.

Bussanich, John, and Nicholas D. Smith, eds. 2013. *The Bloomsbury Companion to Socrates*. London/New Delhi/New York/Sydney: Bloomsbury.

Conard, Mark T., ed. 2007. *The Philosophy of Neo-Noir*. Kentucky: The University Press of Kentucky.

Constable, Catherine. 2004. Postmodernism and Film. In *The Cambridge Companion to Postmodernism*, ed. Steven Connor, 43–61. Cambridge: Cambridge University Press.

Copjec, Joan, ed. 1993. *Shades of Noir: A Reader*. London/New York: Verso.

Dancyger, Ken. 2002. *The Technique of Film and Video Editing: History, Theory, and Practice*. 3rd ed. New York: Focal Press.

Desser, David. 2003. Global Noir: Genre Film in the Age of Transnationalism. In *Film Genre Reader III*, ed. Barry Keith Grant, 516–536. Austin: University of Texas Press.

Dimendberg, Edward, ed. 2004. *Film Noir and the Spaces of Modernity*. Cambridge, MA: Harvard University Press.

Eagleton, Terry. 1987. Estrangement and Irony. *Salmagundi*, Special Issue, Milan Kundera: Fictive Lightness. Fictive Weight, 73 (Winter): 25–32.

Ehrlich, David. 2018. 'The Island' Review: China's Latest Mega-Hit Proves that American Comedies Are Playing Things Too Safe. Posted Aug 24, 2018. https://www.indiewire.com/2018/08/the-island-review-huang-bo-shu-qi-1201997399/. Accessed 21 May 2019.

Evans, Jonathan. 2014. Zhang Yimou's *Blood Simple*: Cannibalism, Remaking and Translation in World Cinema. *Journal of Adaptation in Film & Performance* 7 (3): 283–297.

Farber, Stephen. 1974. Movie Crazy. *The Hudson Review* 27 (2): 252–258.

Fay, Jennifer, and Justus Nieland. 2010. *Film Noir: Hard-Boiled Modernity and Cultures of Globalization*. London/New York: Routledge.

Fluck, Winfried. 2001. Crime, Guilt, and Subjectivity in *Film Noir. Amerikastudien/ American Studies* 46 (3): 379–408.

Foucault, Michel. 2012. *The Courage of Truth: The Government of Self and Others II*. New York: Picador, Palgrave Macmillan.

Foundas, Scott. 2014. Film Review: *Black Coal, Thin Ice*. Posted February 13, 2014. https://variety.com/2014/film/reviews/berlin-film-review-black-coal-thin-ice-1201099676/. Accessed 15 Aug 2019.

Frey, Mattias. 2006. No(ir) Place to Go: Spatial Anxiety and Sartorial Intertextuality in 'Die Unberührbare'. *Cinema Journal* 45 (4): 64–80.

Fusso, Susanne. 1994. *Essays on Gogol: Logos and the Russian Word*. Chicago: Northwestern University Press.

Gao, Minglu. 2003. Post-Utopian Avant-Garde Art in China. In *Postmodernism and the Postsocialist Condition: Politicized Art Under Late Socialism*, ed. Ales Erjavec. Berkeley: University of California Press.

Gleber, Anke. 1998. *The Art of Taking a Walk: Flânerie, Literature, and Film in Weimar Culture*. Princeton: Princeton University Press.

Hassan, Ihab. 1986. Pluralism in Postmodern Perspective. *Critical Inquiry* 12 (3): 503–520.

Hooper, B. 1991. Chinese Youth: The Nineties Generation. *Current History* 90: 264–269.

Hutcheon, Linda. 2002. *The Politics of Postmodernism*. 2nd ed. London/New York: Routledge.

Jameson, Fredric. 1991. *Postmodernism, or, The Cultural Logic of Late Capitalism*. Durham: Duke University Press.

Kolker, Robert. 2000. *A Cinema of Loneliness: Penn, Stone, Kubrick, Scorsese, Spielberg, Altman*. 3rd ed. New York: Oxford University Press.

Kundera, Milan. 1984. *The Unbearable Lightness of Being* (Translated from the Czech by Michael Henry Heim). New York: Harper Perennial.

Kuoshu, Harry. 2002. *Celluloid China: Cinematic Encounters with Culture and Society*. Carbondale/Edwardsville: Southern Illinois University Press.

———. 2011. *Metro Movies: Cinematic Urbanism in Post-Mao China*. Carbondale/Edwardsville: Southern Illinois University Press.

———. 2015. Forrest Gump Becomes a Chinese Film Director: Idealism, Formalism, and an In-between Audience. *Global Studies Journal* 8 (1): 1–11.

Larson, Wendy. 2009. *From Ah Q to Lei Feng: Freud and Revolutionary Spirit in 20th Century China*. Stanford: Stanford University Press.

Lee, Min. 2006. 2 Chinese Boys Lip-Sync Their Way to Web Stardom. Posted October 4, 2006. http://www.seattletimes.com/entertainment/2-chinese-boys-lip-sync-their-way-to-web-stardom/. Accessed 2 July 2016.

Link, Perry. 1994. The Old Man's New China. *New York Review of Books* 9 (June): 31–36.

Lloyd, Genevieve. 1996. *Spinoza and the Ethics*. London/New York: Routledge.

Lu Xun. 1977. *Selected Stories of Lu Hsun*. New York/London: Norton & Company.

Marcuse, Herbert. 1966. *Eros and Civilization: A Philosophical Inquiry into Freud*. Boston: Beacon Press.

Marr, D., and S. Rosen. 1998. Chinese and Vietnamese Youth in the 1990s. *The China Journal* 40: 145–172.

McGrath, Jason. 2008. *Postsocialist Modernity: Chinese Cinema, Literature, and Criticism in the Market Age*. Stanford: Stanford University Press.

McKee, Robert. 1998. *Story: Substance, Structure, Style, and the Principles of Screenwriting*. New York: Methuen.

Moore, Robert L. 2005. Generation *Ku*: Individualism and China's Millennial Youth. *Ethnology* 44 (4): 357–376.

Morrow, Lance. 1992. Folklore in a Box. *Time*, September 21, 50.

Naremore, James. 1995–1996. American Film Noir: The History of an Idea. *Film Quarterly* 49 (2): 12–28.

———. 1998. *More Than Night: Film Noir in Its Contexts*. Berkeley: University of California Press.

———. 2008. *More Than Night: Film Noir in Its Contexts*. Updated and Expanded Edition. Berkeley: University of California Press.

Osno, Evan. 2008. *Crazy English*: The National Scramble to Learn a New Language Before the Olympics. Posted April 28, 2008. www.newyorker.com/magazine/2008/04/28/crazy-english. Accessed 15 Mar 2016.

Pisters, Patricia. 2003. *The Matrix of Visual Culture: Working with Deleuze in Film Theory*. Stanford: Stanford University Press.

Rabinowitz, Paula. 2002. *Black & White & Noir: America's Pulp Modernism*. New York: Columbia University Press.

Renzi, Thomas C. 2012. *Screwball Comedy and Film Noir: Unexpected Connections*. Jefferson: McFarland.

Silbergeld, Jerome. 2004. *Hitchcock with a Chinese Face: Cinematic Doubles, Oedipal Triangles, and China's Moral Voice*. Seattle: University of Washington Press.

Siskel, Gene, and Roger Ebert. 1995. Pulp Faction: The Tarantino Generation. *Pulp Fiction* DVD. Burbank: Buena Vista Home Entertainment.

Sobchack, Vivian. 1998. Lounge Time: Postwar Crises and the Chronotope of Film Noir. In *Reading American Film Genres: History and Theory*, ed. Nick Browne, 129–170. Berkeley: University of California Press.

Spoto, Donald. 1984. *The Dark Side of Genius: The Life of Alfred Hitchcock*. New York: Ballantine Books.

Stables, Kate. 1998. The Postmodern Always Rings Twice: Constructing the Femme Fatale in 90s Cinema. In *Women in Film Noir*, ed. E. Ann Kaplan, 164–182. London: British Film Institute Publishing.

Stoehr, Kevin L. 2006. *Nihilism in Film and Television: A Critical Overview from Citizen Kane to The Sopranos*. Jefferson/London: McFarland & Company.

Tuck, Greg. 2009. Laughter in the Dark: Irony, Black Comedy and Noir in the Films of David Lynch, the Coen Brothers and Quentin Tarantino. In *Neo-Noir*, ed. Mark Bould et al., 152–167. London/New York: Wallflower Press.

Walker, David. 2005. Tarantino, Quentin. In *The Routledge Companion to Postmodernism*, ed. Stuart Sim, 2nd ed. London/New York: Routledge.

Wang, Jennifer Hyland. 2000. A Struggle of Contending Stories: Race, Gender, and Political Memory in *Forrest Gump. Cinema Journal*, 39 (3): 92–115.

Yau, Esther C.M., and Tony Williams, eds. 2017. *Hong Kong Neo-Noir*, Edinburgh Studies in East Asian Film. Edinburgh: Edinburgh University Press.

Zhang, Benzi. 1999. Mapping Carnivalistic Discourse in Japanese American Writing. *MELUS (Multi-Ethnic Literature of the United States)* 24 (4): 19–40.

Zhang, Xudong. 1997. *Chinese Modernism in the Era of Reforms: Cultural Fever, Avant-Garde Fiction, and the New Chinese Cinema*. Durham/London: Duke University Press.

———. 2008. *Postsocialism and Cultural Politics: China in the Last Decade of the Twentieth Century*. Durham/London: Duke University Press.

Zhou, Zuyan. 1994. Carnivalization in *The Journey to the West*: Cultural Dialogism in Fictional Festivity. *Chinese Literature: Essays, Articles, Reviews (CLEAR)* 16: 69–92.

Zinsser, Judith P. 1995. Real History, Real Education, Real Merit—or Why Is *Forrest Gump* So Popular? *Journal of Social History*, Special issue: Social History and the American Political Climate: Problems and Strategies, 29: 91–97.

Zizek, Slavoj. 1989. *The Sublime Object of Ideology*. London/New York: Verso.

———, ed. 1994. *Mapping Ideology*. London/New York: Verso.

FILMOGRAPHY (BY DIRECTORS)

AH GAN (AH GUMP)

Happy (Gao xing, 2009)
Beijing Zongyi Xinghao Cultural Media Co.
Script: Jia Pingwa
Cast: Guo Tao, Huang Bo, Tian Yuan, Feng Shuo

BAI QIULIN

The Second Best (Tianxia di er, 2007)
Zhongbei China Arts, Xingmei Media
Script: Feng Yun, Yang Yi
Cast: Qi Ke (Wang Jinsong), Zhang Mo, Li Yugang, Huang Xiaolei, Zhang Shaohua, Yi Zhen, Li Jie, Rao Xinyu

HUANG BO

Crazy Twins (Fengkuang de xiongdi, 2018)
Sponsored by Kentucky Fried Chicken
Script: Wu Hengming, Wu Jingya, Li Rouxuan, Zhang Zhouting, Song Yujie, Jing Yusang
Cast: Huang Bo

LI KAI

Crazy Foolish Thieves (Fengkuang de chunzei, 2012)
Beijing Mingyang Xingdou Film Media Co.
Script: Cai Dongliang, Wang He, Cheng Xiaoguang, Zhang Hanfeng, Yin Junyi
Cast: Wu Zhenyu (Francis Ng), Lin Xue (Suet Lam), Peng Bo, Ying Er, Wang Taili, Lian Jin (Teddy Lin), Dong Lifan

LIU GUOQUAN

Desperate Songstress (Fengkuang genü), 1988
Inner Mongolia Film Studio
Script: Lin Hongtong, Xiao Mao
Cast: Mao Ahmin, Ma Chongle, Guo Xuxin

MA LIWEN

Lost and Found (Wo jiao Liu Yuejin, 2008)
Beijing Chengtian Zhihong Media Co.
Script: Liu Zhenyun
Cast: Li Yixiang, Liu Xinyi, Liu Hua, Chen Jin, Gao Jun, Qin Hailu

NING HAO

Crazy Stone (Fengkuang de shitou, 2006)
Yingyi Entertainment, Sifang Original International, China Film Huana
  Hengdian Co.
Script: Zhang Cheng, Ning Hao, Yue Xiaojun
Cast: Guo Tao, Liu Hua, Lian Jin, Huang Bo, Xu Zheng
Crazy Racer/Silver Medalist (Fengkuang de saiche, 2009)
Beijing Film Studio, China Film Huana Hengdian Co.
Script: Cui Siwei, Xin Aina, Wang Hongwei, Wang Yao, Zhou Zhiyong, Yue
  Xiaojun, Zhang Cheng
Cast: Huang Bo, Rong Xiang, Jiu Kong, Xu Zheng, Wang Shuangbao
Crazy Alien (Fengkuang de waixing ren, 2019)
Huanxi Media Group, Beijing Dirty Monkey Studio Co. LTD, Beijing Enlight
  Pictures
Script: Sun Xiaohang, Wu Nan, Liu Xiaodan, Pan Yiran, Dong Runnian, Ning
  Hao, Steven Gary Banks, Xing Aina
Cast: Huang Bo, Shen Teng, Xu Zheng, Matthew Morrison, Tom Pelphrey

WANG YUELUN

Almost Perfect (Shi quan jiu mei, 2008)
Beijing Happy Stars Cultural Media Co.
Script: Gao Fei
Cast: Li Weilian, Huang Yi, Liu Hua, Deng Jiajia, Li Yu

ZHANG YIMOU

A Simple Noodle Story (San qiang pai'an jingqi, 2009)
Beijing New Picture Co.
Script: Xu Zhengchao, Shi Jianquan
Cast: Yan Ni, Xiao Shenyang, Sun Honglei, Ni Dahong, Cheng Ye

ZHOU XIAOWEN

Desperation (Zuihou de fengkuang, 1987)
Xi'an Film Studio
Script: Lu Wei, Shi Chenyuan, Shi Chenfeng
Cast: Zhang Jianmin, Liu Xiaoning, Jin Lili
Obsession (Fengkuang de daijia, 1988)
Xi'an Film Studio
Script: Lu Wei, Zhou Xiaowen
Cast: Chang Rong, Li Jing, Wu Yujuan, Xie Yuan, Lin Yongjian

INDEX[1]

[1] Note: Page numbers followed by 'n' refer to notes.

© The Author(s), under exclusive license to Springer Nature
Switzerland AG 2021
H. H. Kuoshu, *Craziness and Carnival in Neo-Noir Chinese
Cinema*, Chinese Literature and Culture in the World,
https://doi.org/10.1007/978-3-030-73081-9

Harry H. Kuoshu
Department of Asian Studies
Furman University
Greenville, SC, USA

Chinese Literature and Culture in the World
ISBN 978-3-030-73080-2   ISBN 978-3-030-73081-9   (eBook)
https://doi.org/10.1007/978-3-030-73081-9

Cover illustration: Pattern © Melisa Hasan

This Palgrave Macmillan imprint is published by the registered company Springer Nature Switzerland AG.
The registered company address is: Gewerbestrasse 11, 6330 Cham, Switzerland

Harry H. Kuoshu

Craziness and Carnival in Neo-Noir Chinese Cinema

palgrave
macmillan

As China is becoming an important player on the world stage, Chinese literature is poised to change and reshape the overlapping, shared cultural landscapes in the world. This series publishes books that reconsider Chinese literature, culture, criticism, and aesthetics in national and international contexts. While seeking studies that place China in geopolitical tensions and historical barriers among nations, we encourage projects that engage in empathetic and learning dialogue with other national traditions. Imbued with a desire for mutual relevance and sympathy, this dialogue aspires to a modest prospect of world culture. We seek theoretically informed studies of Chinese literature, classical and modern - works capable of rendering China's classical heritage and modern accomplishments into a significant part of world culture. We promote works that cut across the modern and tradition divide and challenge the inequality and unevenness of the modern world by critiquing modernity. We look for projects that bring classical aesthetic notions to new interpretations of modern critical theory and its practice. We welcome works that register and analyze the vibrant contemporary scenes in the online forum, public sphere, and media. We encourage comparative studies that account for mutual parallels, contacts, influences, and inspirations.

More information about this series at
http://www.palgrave.com/gp/series/14891

Chinese Literature and Culture in the World

Series Editor
Ban Wang
Stanford University
Stanford, CA, USA